Film Nation

Hollywood Looks at U.S. History

Robert Burgoyne

University of Minnesota Press

Minneapolis

London

Chapter 3 first appeared in a different form in *Screen*, Volume 35, Number 3 (Autumn 1994), used by permission of Oxford University Press. Chapter 4 was originally published in *The Persistence of History*, ed. Vivian Sobchack, used by permission of the publisher, Routledge: New York and London.

Illustrations on pages 62, 64, 65, 72, 74, 75, 76, 83, 107, 110, 111, 112, 113, 115, 116, and 118 courtesy of Photofest.

Published by the University of Minnesota Press
111 Third Avenue South, Suite 290, Minneapolis, MN 55401-2520
http://www.upress.umn.edu
Printed in the United States of America on acid-free paper

Second printing 1998

Library of Congress Cataloging-in-Publication Data

Burgoyne, Robert, 1949–
    Film nation : Hollywood looks at U.S. history / Robert Burgoyne.
        p.   cm.
    Includes index.
    ISBN 0-8166-2070-9 (hardcover : alk. paper). — ISBN 0-8166-2071-7
(pbk. : alk. paper)
    1. Historical films—United States—History and criticism.   2. United States in
motion pictures.   3. Motion pictures and history.   I. Title.
    PN1995.9.H5B87   1997
    791.43'658—dc21   97-5919
                                                                                                     CIP

For my father, Robert Alexander Burgoyne

Contents

Acknowledgments   ix

Introduction   1

1 | Race and Nation in *Glory*   16

2 | Native America, *Thunderheart*, and the National Imaginary   38

3 | National Identity, Gender Identity, and the Rescue Fantasy in *Born on the Fourth of July*   57

4 | Modernism and the Narrative of Nation in *JFK*   88

5 | Prosthetic Memory/National Memory: *Forrest Gump*   104

Conclusion   120

Notes   123

Index   135

Acknowledgments

I would like to extend a special thank-you to my colleagues in film studies at Wayne State University, Lesley Brill, Cynthia Erb, and Corey Creekmur, for their ideas and advice on this project. I would also like to thank Tom Gunning, Vivian Sobchack, Robert Rosenstone, and Hayden White for their encouragement and interest. Tom Conley, once again, gave me invaluable help with this text. For stimulating conversations on nation, memory, and history, I would like to acknowledge my former colleague in film studies, Janet Walker. Thanks also to David Nelson of the Word Processing Center at Wayne State University, whose professionalism and courtesy were equal to the demands I placed upon him. At several points in the research and writing of this text, Wayne State University provided generous assistance in the form of grants and fellowships, for which I am grateful. And most of all, I thank Biodun Iginla, whose faith in this project, and in my work in general, has been steadfast and sustaining.

Introduction

With questions of national, racial, and cultural identity emerging as a central topic of debate in the United States, the American past has become a contested domain in which narratives of people excluded from traditional accounts have begun to be articulated in a complex dialogue with the dominant tradition. One of the most visible manifestations of this changing narrative of nation, a change that is evident throughout the spectrum of contemporary life, can be found in the resurgence of films that take the American past as their subject. Recent films such as *Glory, Thunderheart, JFK, Born on the Fourth of July, Malcolm X, Jefferson in Paris,* and *Forrest Gump* bring into relief the striking degree to which the national narrative is currently being reshaped by stories that explore the meaning of nation "from below." Although occasionally flawed by nostalgia and by a somewhat glancing relation to the historical record, these films illuminate what I think is a pervasive and growing tendency in contemporary American culture: the desire to remake what the sociologist Jacques Rancière has called the "dominant fiction," the ideological reality or "image of social consensus" within which members of a society are asked to identify themselves.[1] This impulse permeates present-day culture; even Disney's plans for a theme park on American history, for example, emphasize the importance of representing the experiences of racial and ethnic minorities, including slavery and industrial exploitation, as central aspects of the American past. But the leading edge of this impulse, in my

1

view, is the cinematic rewriting of history currently taking shape, which stands as a particularly conspicuous attempt to rearticulate the cultural narratives that define the American nation. By interrogating the reserve of images and stories that constitute the dominant fiction, these films set forth a counternarrative of American history that ultimately attempts to reinforce social belief.

In describing the concept of the dominant fiction, Rancière emphasizes the importance of narrative and pictorial forms, particularly films, in fostering a sense of national identity, arguing that they create an "image of society immediately readable by all classes."[2] In this regard, his discussion, dating from 1977, anticipates many of the most recent analyses of nationalism, which typically emphasize the importance of narrative forms in creating concepts of nation; as Timothy Brennan writes, the idea of nation depends on "an apparatus of cultural fictions."[3] The link between national identity and narrative is especially apparent in the American cinema, Rancière suggests, in which the dominant fiction of "the birth of the nation" is replayed in different ways: "whites versus Indians; North versus South; Law versus outlaw, etc." In my view, however, what Rancière admiringly calls "the legend of the formation of the code" is in the process of being transformed. Rather than rehearsing the foundational narrative that Rancière summarizes as "this is where we come from," contemporary historical films seek, on the whole, to recover a different message from the past, a message that will validate the increasingly hybrid and polycultural reality of American life and bind it to an image of nation that expresses a sense of "this is how we are."[4]

In combining the viewpoints of dominant and nondominant peoples, however, these films also register another more difficult and disturbing theme, which I will call "identity from across." The films I treat in this study insistently return to a certain hard kernel of historical truth—that social identities in the United States have largely been shaped by relations of opposition and antagonism, and that fear and hatred of the other have exerted just as powerful an influence on the molding of ethnic and racial identity as the positive and organic traits that supposedly distinguish one group from another. The stories of nation that these films unfold convey a strong sense of the way white identity, for example, has shaped itself in contrast to its perceptions of black identity, or the way American "civilization" has defined itself in contrast to conceptions of Indian "savagery"—an oppositional logic that works against the idea that nationalism can be reconceived and re-configured to express new forms of social coherence.[5]

I offer the concept of identity from across as a way of foregrounding the agonistic, contestatory character of this rewriting of the dominant fiction. Far from viewing national identity in terms of what theorists have described as a "deep, horizontal comradeship," an "imagined community" characterized by social unisonance, recent films dealing with the American past frequently address the fundamental contradiction at the center of the narrative of nation—the contradiction posed by race.[6] The stark inconsistency between national ideals of a deep, horizontal comradeship and the actuality of racial hierarchy and oppression, what Virginia Wright Wexman calls the tension between "the ideal of a community of equals and the drive for domination by groups within the culture," has been explored with surprising directness in certain contemporary films.[7] Works such as *Thunderheart*, *Malcolm X*, and *Glory*, for example, throw into relief the subtle and complex antagonisms that structure identity in America—most evident in the way white and black American identities, for example, have been shaped in a relation of contrast and, in some cases, a relation of mimicry with each other. Social identity, as conceived in these films, originates neither from "above," in alignment with the nation-state, nor from below, with ethnicity or race, but rather from "across," through horizontal relations whose antagonistic and transitive character is best represented in terms of "inside" and "outside."[8] The mythology of national identity in the United States, as recent films suggest, thus harbors a double contradiction: not only is the ideal of deep, horizontal comradeship belied by the fact of racial hierarchy and domination, but the myth of nation is also contradicted by a kind of lateral caste system, in which identity is constructed in relations of opposition and, occasionally, imitation "from across."

Because these films confront what I feel are the most important and complex issues in American life today, the ongoing controversy over the legitimacy of cinematic interpretations of the past, a controversy that reached a critical flashpoint with *JFK* and *Malcolm X* and that flared again over *Jefferson in Paris* and *Nixon*, to my mind misses the point and at the same time reveals the significance of the stakes on the table. The argument over film's responsibility to the past encompasses several distinct issues. Perhaps the most vexing concern, for many, is the preeminent role that film has assumed in interpreting the past for contemporary society. The influence of film on present-day historical consciousness and understanding has often been described as debilitating; an important counterargument has been raised, however, in connection with the increasing absorption of mainstream films and television programs with the American past. Describing this phenomenon as a positive revitalization of "social memory," the historian Michael Kammen argues that the popularity of historical films and television movies, of historical theme parks and the rage for Americana in decorating and architecture—even the use of historical allusions in advertising—are part of a widespread trend that he calls "the emotional discovery of America."[9] Assessing both the limits and the strengths of this mass diffusion of interest, Kammen argues that the contemporary period is uniquely characterized by a dualistic relation to the past. The 1980s were especially noteworthy, in his view, as a time of "surging public interest in the past, but also a time when ignorance of United States history proved to be astounding; a time when spurious traditions were concocted and commercialized, but also a time when vernacular arts and folk culture flourished as never before."[10] Kammen views this paradox as a consequence of the split between history and memory in the contemporary United States. Memory and history, he writes, are peculiarly fractured and joined to one another in American culture—fractured because of the social diversity that gives us a multitude of memories, rather than a single, monolithic cultural memory; joined because the "genuine intermingling of cultures" that characterizes our contemporary reality gives us a history that "hinges on memory."[11] Unofficial forms of collective rememoration, including film and television programs based on historical subjects, have thus become increasingly important in the 1980s and 1990s in terms of their visibility and in terms of their influence on emerging and traditional concepts of collective identity.[12]

A similar argument for the persistence of collective memory in commercial, popular forms is offered by George Lipsitz, who sets forth an intriguing approach to social memory based on what he calls a "sedimented layer of historical knowledge and historical critique" in popular culture artifacts.[13] Commercial culture, he argues, can function as a site of opposition and resistance precisely insofar as it depends and draws upon actual historical experiences and traditions. Ethnic and class memories, for example, may be distorted and trivialized in commercial culture, but there are nonetheless historically specific elements within commercial culture that represent an expression of collective popular memory and the reworking of tradition that can be activated on behalf of social change. Popular culture—and his examples range from television programs of the 1950s to Mardi Gras songs and costumes—when viewed as an evocation of collective memory and tradition, however much transformed, conveys a form of contemporary social engagement with history that is usually overlooked: "The desire to connect to history, the impulse to pose present problems in historical terms, and the assertion of a temporal and social reality beyond one's immediate experience pervade popular culture."[14] Lipsitz offers the striking conclusion that popular memory, tradition, and knowledge exist not just in the fading memories of marginalized groups, but in the strongholds of the contemporary economy.

A second issue that often arises in these discussions is the interpenetration of history by fiction in contemporary films. The erosion of the presumed boundary between factual and fictional discourses has been the subject of much anguished commentary, with films that focus on the historical past sometimes held to standards of authenticity and verifiability that nearly equal the standards applied to scholarly historical texts. As Caryn James reminds us, however, in a powerful defense of the history film, "Such responses naively assume that an accumulation of facts equals truth. But a collection of facts is no more than an almanac. History is the interpretation of those facts."[15] The seemingly absolute border between imaginative and realistic discourses is necessarily permeable, for historical writing delivers not the "real" of the historical past but rather a mental conception of it, a system of discursive representations, in which speculation, hypothesis, and dramatic ordering and shaping closely inform the work of historical reconstruction and analysis. Moreover, dramatic license and a strong point of view are essential for these films to work as art, or to claim a share of the social power and influence that inheres in storytelling, both fictional and historical. James argues that social power and influence are in fact the real issue here, the one that is most troubling to critics of historical films; these films are controversial, she writes, not because of their intermingling of fiction and history, but because of their "use of fiction to challenge history's accepted views."[16]

Indeed, in works such as *Glory, JFK, Born on the Fourth of July, Thunderheart,* and *Forrest Gump,* the national past appears to be a story with distinctly tragic overtones; the narrative of nation these films convey is at least partially a narrative of collective loss. Seen in the most positive light, they appear to be engaged in the task described by the anthropologist Victor Turner as "remaking cultural sense." Turner writes that "where historical life itself fails to make cultural sense in terms that formerly held good, narrative and cultural dramas may have the task of poesis, that is, of remaking cultural sense, even when they seem to be dismantling ancient edifices of meaning."[17] Joining a formidable quality of social criticism to a newly libidinalized national narrative, recent historical films can be seen as part of the ongoing revisionary enterprise of the late twentieth century; they reenact the narrative of nation in terms of its tributaries, in terms of stories of ethnic, racial, and gender struggles to reshape the national narrative, and to make the experiences of marginal groups a "formative and necessary part of the story."[18]

It is precisely the reshaping of our collective imaginary relation to history, and to nation, that I explore in this text. Issues such as cinema's ostensible distortion of historical reality or of the culture's willingness to substitute glossy images for historical understanding and insight are ultimately secondary to the more pointed challenge that recent historical films convey—their challenge to the traditional myths of the nation-state. The films I have chosen to examine bring into relief issues of power that underlie the idealized construction of nationhood, exposing the "fissures and faultlines" between national myths and the historical experiences of people excluded from dominant accounts.[19] Debates about film and its responsibility to the past largely obscure what I think are more significant issues—the central position occupied by film in the articulation of national identity and film's ability to hold up to scrutiny and drive home the emotional meaning of the imagined community of nation and its bruising inadequacies.

In its range and coverage of the field of national imaginings, the Hollywood cinema is in many ways an unparalleled expression of national culture, one that has molded the self-image of the nation in pervasive and explicit ways. Presumably because it functions independently of state support or government guidelines, however, the Hollywood cinema is generally not considered under the rubric of national cinema; nevertheless, it unambiguously articulates an imaginary field in which the figures of national identification are deployed and projected. Concepts of social reality constructed in Hollywood films clearly serve as legitimating discourses in the life of the nation, a function that is particularly visible in the way the national past is represented in mainstream American films.[20]

In the contemporary period, however, many of the most hallowed myths of nation have been challenged and criticized in feature films that contest the basic premises of American ideology—the myth of manifest destiny, for example, or of the progressive extension of liberty to ever-increasing numbers of people, or of the power of national belonging to displace the lived identity of race, or of the existence of a single, homogeneous nation extending from "sea to shining sea." Even within mainstream Hollywood filmmaking, the foundational narratives of nation are increasingly being contested by films that open up the locked doors of the national past and that emphasize the histories forgotten or excluded from dominant accounts.

Nevertheless, the cinematic rewriting of history that is currently unfolding retains elements of what one writer aptly calls "the relic imaginary of the past."[21] Despite highly critical messages concerning the national past, the films that form the core of this study preserve and revivify some of the basic tropes of traditional narratives of nation—the image of a mystic nationhood that is revealed only on the battlefield, for example, or the importance of warfare in molding a sense of ethnic and national community. The discourse of national identity in the works I analyze, although radically reconfigured by their focus on the struggles of people outside the circuits of power, is nonetheless drawn from a filmic lexicon that is filled with powerful, emotionally charged images of martial conflict. Drawing on what Mikhail Bakhtin calls the "genre memory" of the western, the war film, and the melodrama, the texts I examine here set up a complex dialogue between the sedimented memories of history and nation preserved in these genre forms and the alternative narratives of historical experience they bring into relief.[22]

Bakhtin's concept of genre memory provides a way of approaching one of the most remarkable aspects of these films: the fact that their appeal to new forms of social coherence is to a large extent shaped by the rhetoric, imagery, and genre patterning of what might well be called the war myths of the national past. Although a great deal of recent scholarship on nationalism and national identity has emphasized the roles of the novel, the newspaper, and film in creating the imagined community of the modern nation, many of these influential approaches overlook what I take to be one of the most significant and obvious forms of national mythology: the war stories of the nation-state.[23] In the twentieth-century United States, the narrative forms that have molded national identity most profoundly are arguably the western and the war film, genres that articulate an image of nation that, in the words of Anthony D. Smith, has been "beaten into national shape by the hammer of incessant wars."[24]

Now these genre forms, as Bakhtin argues, impose their own historical perspectives and systems of value on individual texts, even those that employ generic codes in nontraditional ways. Capable of both recalling past usages and responding to the present in a new way, genres serve as the principal vehicles for shaping and carrying social experience from one generation to another. Understood as crystallized forms of social and cultural memory, genres may be seen as "organs of memory" that embody the worldview of the period from which they originated while carrying with them "the layered record of their changing use." As Morson and Emerson write in their recent book on Bakhtin, "Genres are the residue of past behavior . . . the crystallization of earlier interactions . . . congealed events." They both "resume past usage . . . and redefine present experience in an additional way." They "remember the past, and make their resources and potentials available to the present."[25]

Born on the Fourth of July, Thunderheart, Glory, JFK, and *Forrest Gump* draw on the genre memory of the western, the war film, and the melodrama in ways that evoke what Smith calls "the fund of accumulated myths and images common to the community";[26] they do so, however, in a way that Bakhtin has described as "double-voicing"—the adapting of an older genre to a new context. Although these films appear to be reiterating positions that are fundamental to the most traditional forms of nationalism—setting forth the conditions "under which force or violence is justified in a people's defense"—the most salient and significant message that emerges from them is their call to defend a concept of nation that has all too often eschewed the power of what one writer calls "blood arguments."[27] In my efforts to come to grips with the seemingly contradictory messages of these films—their embrace of an expanded social vision and an enlarged sense of national community, together with their dramatic assertions of a kind of blood rhetoric that communicates a potent, even militant, national self-image—I have been led to consider the distinction between ethnic and civic nationalism discussed by Michael Ignatieff in *Blood and Belonging* and by Anthony D. Smith in his recent book, *National Identity*.[28]

Civic nationalism, Ignatieff writes, "maintains that the nation should be composed of all those—regardless of race, color, creed, gender, language, or ethnicity—who subscribe to the nation's political creed. This nationalism is called civic because it envisages the nation as a community of equal, rights-bearing citizens, united in patriotic attachment to a shared set of political practices and values." Ethnic nationalism, on the other hand, maintains that what gives unity to the nation, what makes it a place of passionate attachment, is "not the cold contrivance of shared rights but the people's preexisting ethnic characteristics: their language, religion, customs and traditions. . . . that an individual's deepest attachments are inherited, not chosen."[29] Smith points out that conceptually, the nation is a blend of these two dimensions, "the one civic and territorial, the other ethnic and genealogical," in varying proportions in particular cases, and that it is this "very multidimensionality that has made national identity such a flexible and persistent force in modern life."[30]

In my view, *Thunderheart, Born on the Fourth of July, Glory*, and *JFK* are engaged in the project of defining a new form of civic nationalism, a kind of "polycentric" or "pluralistic" nationalism, which can be seen as an alternative to the virulent ethnic or ethnocentric nationalism so prevalent today—a reversion to a form of tribalism that has begun to assert itself in the United States in the form of the white militia movement.[31] Ignatieff underlines the need to defend this form of national identity: "Liberal civilization—the rule of laws, not men, of argument in place of force, of compromise in place of violence—runs deeply against the human grain and is achieved and sustained only by the most unremitting struggle against human nature. The liberal virtues—tolerance, compromise, reason—remain as valuable as ever, but they cannot be preached to those who are mad with fear or mad with vengeance. . . . We must be prepared to defend them by force."[32] In the films I consider here, the defense of nation, conceived more or less on the civic model described by Ignatieff, forms a central, unifying theme, offering a strong sense of the power of blood arguments to crystallize a sense of national purpose; as one writer says, to "force a social alignment, to force a decision about a social truth."[33]

The more inclusive, alternative social narratives set forth by these films are thus irrigated by the rhetoric of bloodshed and by stories of "blood sacrifices for nation."[34] As Ignatieff reminds us, civic nationalism is the only effective antidote to ethnic nationalism; civic nationalism, however, appears also to require the "ennobling" rhetoric of blood myths. Thus, the narrative of nation survives in works such as *Born on the Fourth of July*, *Glory*, and *JFK*, but in a changed form; instead of the story of an original grandeur that has continued unbroken into the present, these films convey the social ruptures of the Vietnam decade and the Civil War as openings to another, emergent narrative, similar to what Homi Bhabha calls a "hybrid national narrative," constructed from histories that have been excluded from traditional accounts.[35] These films suggest that there are potentially many histories embedded in a given historical moment, histories that may be plural and conflicting, and that require different constructions of the national past. Out of these plural and conflicting histories, we may begin to glimpse the outline of the pluralistic or polycentric form of national identity defined by Smith and the Israeli writer Yael Tamir.

My approach to these films can also be seen as a kind of implicit argument against the presumption that the nation form is fading as a dominant focus of identification. Recently, several influential theorists have argued that the category of the nation has been superseded by the globalization of economies and by the spread of information technologies, that national boundaries have been effectively dissolved. Social, cultural, and economic life in the late twentieth century, the argument goes, is increasingly organized in transnational ways; real power is draining away from the nation-state, and it is only at the political level that the nation-state retains its identity. Yet the importance of the imagined community of nation in the cultural and emotional life of even the most cosmopolitan societies should not be dismissed. Ignatieff makes the case that our deepest allegiances and affiliations are hardly touched by the apparatuses and insignia of global systems:

> Our identities are based on the small symbols that differentiate us. Freud called this "the narcissism of minor difference." It does not matter how small the difference is; we can make it into the core of our identity. Cosmopolitans keep expecting Levi's and Benetton, McDonald's and IBM to erode these minor differences. All that happens is that people cling more tenaciously to the deeper differences that remain. Yugoslavia was filled with sophisticated Europeans, driving Mercedes cars and owning Swiss-style chalets. On the outside, one could not tell them apart. On the inside they remained Croats,

Serbs, and Bosnian Muslims. Yugoslavia shows how little modernization touches our deepest allegiances.[36]

Here I would like to defend the discourse of nation as a viable and strategic category of analysis—the nation seen not as the repository of a unitary, immutable, and essentialized identity, but rather as the basis of critique, the basis for interrogating and exposing the relations of power that lie at the heart of the idea of nation, and for making audible the oppositional voices that "cohabit the national space."[37] Although narratives of nation are traditionally chauvinist, narrow, and conservative, the category of nation, as Iain Chambers puts it, is not a closed history, something already achieved: rather, it can be seen as an open framework, as something continually in the making.[38] And, as the Australian critic Graeme Turner reminds us, "We should not assume that the battle for the discourses of the nation are over, or finalized."[39]

Despite the difficulty of conceiving nationalism in terms of polycentric or pluralistic modalities, I feel it is strategically unwise to shift the struggle onto less difficult terrain. In a period when armed militias in the United States have begun a campaign of white ethnic nationalism that threatens to rend the civic form of nationalism that has defined the American ideal for centuries, despite its limitations in practice, the power of mainstream films to articulate the more elusive and somewhat inchoate desire for new forms of social coherence, for a new national vision based on the polycultural reality of American life, should be recognized as a positive cultural force. The contemporary historical film is, in this sense, a privileged discursive site in which anxiety, ambivalence, and expectation about the nation, its history, and its future are played out in narrative form. What I try to stress in the chapters that follow is the way the cinematic rewriting of history currently unfolding articulates a counternarrative of nation that, paradoxically, throws into relief the power and importance of concepts of national belonging, a form of belonging conceived not on the narrow, ethnic model of blood and origins, but rather on the model of a civic pluralism that holds that "a nation should be a home to all, and race, color, religion and creed should be no bar to belonging."[40] As these films demonstrate, in the inherited language of genres such as the western, the war film, and the male melodrama, this concept has in the past been forcefully defended. In their coupling of pointed social criticism

with an overtly emotional appeal to the value of national consciousness and national identity, these films reinforce Nathan Huggins's call
for a new national narrative that will be "vastly more coherent, logi-
cal, and inclusive" and that will "reflect upon our true condition . . . as
having a common story, and necessarily sharing the same fate."[41]

The five films this study comprises offer complex and sophisticated
treatments of the linked themes of nationhood and history. Each of
these texts interrogates the historical basis and the changing character
of national identity in the United States from a different perspective,
and together they offer a kind of "portrait in the round" of what can
be called the "national imaginary" in the contemporary period.[42] In
each, the nation is portrayed at a moment of historical crisis—the Civil
War in *Glory*, the Vietnam War in *Born on the Fourth of July*, the assassination of John F. Kennedy in *JFK*, the centuries-old struggle between the state and Native America that *Thunderheart* revisits in the
context of the aftermath of the siege of Wounded Knee in the 1970s,
and the 1960s of *Forrest Gump*. The defining moments of American
history, these films suggest, are those that force the margins into the
center of the national text and that compel a new configuration of the
nation's self-image.

Although these five films could hardly be said to exhaust the range
of issues and contradictions circulating through and around the concept of nation in the present day, the texts I have chosen represent several points of an imaginary compass that allows for a fairly accurate
survey of the intellectual and historical field of national identity. The
cardinal concepts and ideas concerning nationalism in the contemporary period are dramatized here in narratives replete with symbolism,
myth, history, and drama, in which the crises and conflicts of an increasingly multicultural society are translated into the discourse of vernacular and national mobilization. Each of these films allows me to
address different facets of the question of national identity, and each
brings into view previously unmarked areas of history, ideology, and
cultural life.

In chapter 1, I consider the Civil War film *Glory* in terms of the
competing forces of race and national construction. In articulating the
historical construction of racial identity at a moment when concepts of
nation are once again undergoing radical redefinition, *Glory* conveys
a particularly complex understanding of the way racial and cultural

identity is bound up with the national narrative. Drawing on the distinction Cornel West makes between identity from above (identification with the nation-state) and identity from below (racial and ethnic identity), I show how the struggle for racial visibility and recognition that culminates in the spectacular assault and massacre of the film's final sequence is complicated by another, competing message. In counterpoint to the ostensible subject matter and theme of the film, which might be defined in humanistic terms as the mutual reshaping and redefinition of identity from below and identity from above, the film also explores the more fractious subject of the failure of social movements to cut across racial identities, emphasizing the fear and hatred of the other as the constant feature of national experience. In its unusually direct examination of what I call identity from across—the particularities of white and black identity defined in relation to one another—the film makes evident the limits of its own nationalist solution to racial difference and antagonism, projecting in its closing images not a triumphal story of social progress but rather a national story that is in part a collective narrative of social loss.

Chapter 2 focuses on the film *Thunderheart* as an example of the changing image of Native Americans in the "national imaginary" of the nation-state. Here, I consider the way Native Americans have emerged in contemporary films as agents of a powerful counternarrative of nation, bearers of an alternative historical and national consciousness molded and shaped by centuries of incessant war. The theme of continuous struggle against the nation-state is expressed visually in the film's striking opening sequence, which fashions a reversal of the territorial imaginary of the state, calling into question the dominant metaphor of east-west "progress" and the basic model of history underpinning the master narrative of nation. However, I also note the ways *Thunderheart* draws on what Bakhtin calls the genre memory of the western, historically one of the nation-state's most important vehicles of nationalist ideology. The historical signals and cultural values associated with the western interpenetrate and affect the construction of new images in *Thunderheart* in ways that suggest an affinity between the two nations.

Chapter 3 looks at the film *Born on the Fourth of July* as a complicated variant of what Susan Jeffords calls "the remasculinization of America."[43] Linking the symbolism of nationalism to the iconography of gender in an overt way, the film anatomizes the failure of masculinist national ideals in the Vietnam period, offering in its closing scenes an alternative image of nation based on the metaphor of a maternal, social body America, an "America who can embrace all her children." But while the film overturns myths of masculinity constructed on ideals of "punitive agency," it restores the privileged place of the male hero by appealing to another cultural paradigm, what Freud called "the rescue fantasy" in which the male hero gains authority by "rescuing" the nation, figured as a woman, from its own weakness. In its portrait of the Vietnam veteran as victim of patriarchy on the one hand and as savior of the nation on the other, *Born on the Fourth of July* solicits a more complex reading of masculine agency in the Vietnam film than has been given to date.

In chapter 4, I examine the film *JFK* in terms of the tension between the film's formal innovations and its explicit aim to articulate a narrative of national cohesion. Contrasting the film's fragmentary, atomized form to the sense of simultaneity and connectedness that Benedict Anderson maintains is crucial to the imagined community of the modern nation, I argue that the film's profusion of stylistic modes and idioms expresses the rupture of a once-unified national text. In its collagelike structure, *JFK* calls to mind the idea set forth recently by Hayden White—that modernist, antinarrative techniques, characterized by fragmentation, the exploding of the conventions of the traditional tale, and the dissociation or splitting of narrative functions, may be the most appropriate techniques for representing the historical reality of the contemporary period.[44]

In chapter 5, I consider *Forrest Gump* as an example of the powerful role that social memory plays in constructing concepts of nation. The film places in relief the power of memory and narratives of memory to create subjective connections to the national past, to call forth the sense of "I" and "we" that makes the national narrative compelling and meaningful. At the same time, however, the film repudiates the political movements of the 1960s, wiping the slate clean of blacks, women, and the counterculture in an effort to disengage cultural memory from public history. In severing history—understood as the register of public events outside the spectrum of individual experience—from what it envisions as the authentic texture of national life, the film creates a kind of prosthetic memory of the period, refunctioning the cultural memory of the sixties so that it can be integrated into the traditional narrative of nation. It thus imagines America as a kind of virtual nation whose historical debts have been forgiven and whose disabilities have all been corrected.

Each of the films examined here defines national belonging in terms of a complex interplay between what Rancière calls the dominant fiction and local, vernacular memories of adversity and struggle. Each places in relief the wider significance of little-known strands of historical experience. But their most powerful and resonant appeal is their call to defend the concept of civic nationalism in a period when ethnic and racial conflict in the United States has again forced a re-evaluation of the meaning of national belonging. The past speaks to the present with extreme clarity on this particular subject; the films that constitute this study serve the exemplary role of making these lessons audible.

1 | Race and Nation in *Glory*

In resurrecting the forgotten story of a black Union Army regiment and its white leader, Colonel Robert Gould Shaw, *Glory* conveys a particularly complex understanding of the way racial and cultural identity is both bound up with and competes with the forces of national construction. Examining the historical construction of racial and national identity in the United States at a moment when concepts of nation were being fundamentally redefined, *Glory* emphasizes the tension between a civic ideal of nation conceived as a community of equals and the powerful appeal of ethnic and racial identities based on what Michael Ignatieff calls "blood and belonging."[1] Far from mediating or subduing ethnic concepts of nation, the Civil War, the film suggests, pulled potent structures of racial identification into visibility, promoting a sense of racial mobilization in white as well as in black America. *Glory* thus departs from the traditional themes of Civil War narratives, which typically focus on the emancipation of the slaves and the rebirth of national ideals of community and equality, to explore a subject that D. W. Griffith first considered from a rather different perspective: the struggle between competing ideals of nation, ethnic and civic, and their equally potent claims to recognition and belonging.

At first glance, *Glory* appears to be primarily concerned with the relation between what Cornel West has described as identity from above—identification with the nation-state—and identity from below—racial and ethnic identity. These two forms of identity, as West points out, are both defined by the most elemental concerns; they are fundamentally about desire and death. The desire for affiliation, for recognition, for visibility, is one of the most significant and visceral forces shaping both national and racial identity. But the construction of identity also involves the recognition of death, being willing to die for that identity, or being willing to kill others for it.[2] In *Glory*, this concept is dramatized in a strikingly literal way, as the struggle for racial visibility and recognition culminates in the spectacular assault and massacre of the film's final sequence, foregrounding the almost suicidal costs of aligning identity from below and identity from above. Underlining the theme of collective martyrdom with the sounds of choral music, the film idealizes the sacrifice of the black soldiers as the price of national affiliation, as if identity from above were in some way a mystical compact, authorized and conferred only in death. By invoking what Paul Gilroy calls "a mystic nationhood that [is] only revealed on the battlefield," the film further suggests that racial difference is dissolved in warfare, valorizing war as the defining moment when racial and national self-realization coalesce.[3]

But this thesis, in which national identity is presumed to dominate and displace the lived identity of race, is complicated by another, competing message in *Glory*. In counterpoint to the ostensible subject matter and theme of the film, which might be summarized in humanistic terms as the mutual reshaping and redefinition of identity from below and identity from above, the film also explores the more fractious subject of the failure of social movements to cut across racial identities, emphasizing the fear and hatred of the other as the constant feature of national experience. Although the central importance of national identity is asserted strenuously in the closing moments of the film, the body of the text seems to be concerned mainly with what I am calling identity from across: the nonsymmetrical relationship between white identity and black identity that defines points of tension in *Glory* that have little to do with the unifying rhetoric of nation or the traditional Civil War topics of liberty, equality, and self-determination. And it is here that the film illuminates the hard kernel of historical truth that is slowly working its way through the various revisions of the dominant fiction that are currently being offered: the recognition that the achievement of new forms of collective coherence will require something other than an updated narrative of nation, and that only a historical narrative that, as the historian Peter Dimock writes, "is explicitly a collective

narrative of social loss" will be able to address the present crisis of social belief.[4]

This secondary theme is articulated chiefly through the story of the white commanding officer, Colonel Robert Shaw, which serves in large part as a means of registering the dissonance between white racial identity and the imagined community implied by emancipation. Rather than merging whiteness and nation into a single myth, the film suggests that the historical coalescence of black identity during the Civil War forced apart the formerly seamless narrative of white identity, separating it from its traditional one-to-one correspondence with the concept of nation. With emancipation redefining the meaning of national community, the voice of white racial privilege could no longer be heard as the exclusive voice of national ideals. By inverted yet strangely similar paths, *Glory* comes to the same conclusion as D. W. Griffith's *Birth of a Nation*: white identity is defined and clarified by black identity, which forces "whiteness" into the open and compels it to speak in a language of its own.

As Richard Dyer has explained, white identity is an exceptionally elusive and difficult subject to analyze, for it represents itself not in terms of particular characteristics and practices, but rather as a synthesis of all the attributes of humanity. "The strength of white representation . . . [is] the sense that being white is coterminous with the endless plenitude of human diversity."[5] Just as the color itself is defined as a combination of all the other colors, white racial identity seems to have no substance of its own: "White power secures its dominance by seeming not to be anything in particular . . . as if it is the natural, inevitable, ordinary way of being human."[6] The invisibility of whiteness, its lack of specificity, masks it as a category; so thoroughly identified with the norm, white racial identity becomes difficult, especially for white people, to see and to represent.

One of the ways white identity does become visible, Dyer suggests, is in the contrast between white and nonwhite in narratives marked by ethnic or racial difference, narratives in which nonwhite characters play significant roles. In order to represent white identity, a "comparative element" seems to be required, for "only non-whiteness can give whiteness any substance." In such texts, the characteristics of whiteness can be inferred if not defined, understood by way of contrast with the stereotypes associated with nonwhite modes of behavior. In the films Dyer analyzes, the "presence of black people . . . allows one to see whiteness as whiteness." And the sense of whiteness is accentuated, Dyer notes, in films centering on situations where white domination is contested.[7]

These ideas offer an instructive approach to the representation of racial identity in *Glory*. The film uses the drama of the 54th Massachusetts Infantry, the first black regiment to be raised in the North, partly to pull white identity into visibility, detailing the practices and characteristics of the white Union military, emphasizing the "psychology" of whiteness, as seen through Shaw, and placing in relief the internal complacency and self-interest of the white establishment. The effective display of white identity, however, depends on a relation of rigid contrast with black identity, a contrast that recalls the absolute binarisms of racist thought. Stiff formality, an emphasis on individual agency and responsibility, and links to historical tradition are set out as clear markers of whiteness and explicitly set against the exuberance, collectivity, and sense of historical emergence that characterize the black soldiers. In keeping with the film's liberal themes and contemporary perspective, however, many of the features associated with whiteness are held up to scrutiny and subjected to criticism, partly through the voice-overs of Shaw himself. Ultimately, however, the traits identified as white are restored to dominance as Shaw overcomes self-doubt and gains the approbation and respect of the black troops.

As Dyer observes, the ability to resolve this kind of crisis of identity can also be seen as one of the attributes of whiteness; here, the hero restores his own fading sense of authority by appropriating the emotional intensity associated with the black soldiers, displaying an uncharacteristic passion in a series of scenes in which Shaw ferociously confronts the military establishment, dresses down his own officers, and, in an expression of solidarity with his troops, rips up his pay voucher to protest the unequal pay the soldiers have received, taking his cue directly from the black soldier Trip. In a subtle way, however, the emotional intensity common to the black soldiers is recoded in these scenes as part of human nature, latent but still accessible to the white Colonel Shaw. In contrast, when the black soldiers take on the rigor and discipline associated with the whites, it is a cultural attitude, not nature, that is absorbed. Where Shaw seems to require an infusion of natural passion to complete his character, the black soldiers require, in the logic of the film, the armature of certain cultural values associated with whites. Here, the film appears to reiterate conventional notions of blacks possessing more "nature" than whites, whereas whites command the sphere of culture. Thus, despite the superficial impression the film gives of a fluid crossing over of characteristics, the overall marking of racial differences is such that the boundary between black and white appears to be more fixed than permeable, and where mutual reshaping of identities does occur, the traits that are exchanged often play into well-worn stereotypes of racial difference.

Glory provides an especially good map of contemporary liberal thinking about race. In stressing the ways that white identity has been historically conferred, the film displays with exceptional precision the traditions, psychology, and behavior and practices of the white establishment during the Civil War period, underscoring the different ways whiteness, in both its progressive and reactionary aspects, has been shaped by the reality of an emergent black racial identity. In contrast, however, the film offers a portrait of black identity that is affirmative, but resolutely ahistorical, as if black history had to be remade by white hands and according to white ideas in order to release its most powerful messages.[8] Despite the positive accent the story of the black troops receives, the film's erasure of its actual historical figures, compared with its detailed reconstruction of the milieu of

Colonel Shaw, ensures that the relations of racial identity here remain nonsymmetrical.

In general, the film uses two different paradigms to define racial identity, one of which is historical, the other folkloric and stereotypical, which are folded together or superimposed upon one another throughout the film. At several points in the narrative, the particularities of historical experience assert themselves in a powerful fashion, conveying a clear message that history has shaped racial identity in incommensurably different ways. For example, the film foregrounds the different meanings that blacks and whites assign to features of military life and specifically to the war against the Confederacy: military training and discipline, marching, and the climactic battle itself are viewed from a bifocal perspective that makes explicit the distinct optics that racial difference confers. At other points, however, this self-aware and careful dialogical principle gives way to a simple binarism in which racial difference is defined not in terms of historical experience but in terms of intrinsic differences, a tendency that rehearses essentialist patterns of racial representation. Seen in the most positive light, the film makes visible the way identity is constructed transitively, from across, using the binarisms of racial representation in a critical fashion and drawing from the dialogic encounter of black and white a reconsideration of the issues and traditions of national identity. But from another angle, the film hews uncomfortably close to old stereotypes, especially in its folkloric approach to black identity, which diminishes the actual historicity of black experience and identity.

In the pages that follow, I analyze the representation of racial identity in *Glory* from three different perspectives. First, I notice the contrast in the way the participants in the drama are defined and authenticated, a contrast that can be broadly described as historical versus folkloric. Second, I show how the film, despite its occasional lapses into stereotype, extends the dialogic principle discussed above—the foregrounding of the distinct viewpoints that racial difference entails—to encompass the historical process itself, represented in terms of two distinct historical trajectories, two competing narratives of history that are brought into conjunction in the imagery of the road and the march into the South. Third, I consider the messages the film conveys about racial identity and the national narrative from the perspective of the present, arguing that its seemingly traditional message of military valor and sacrifice opening up the "iron gate" to equality is counteracted by another message, signified by the closing shot of bootless corpses, which projects, like a kind of afterimage, a narrative of a nation imprisoned by its past as much as empowered by it.[9]

History versus Folklore

By placing difference and conflict at the center of the national narrative, the film's approach to racial and national identity substantially changes the meaning of the story as it was known in the nineteenth century. Celebrated as one of the most renowned figures of the Civil War, Shaw, along with the 54th Infantry, had captured the imagination of the general public as well as the interest of the literary and political leaders of the period. Shaw's posthumous stature was such that Ralph Waldo Emerson and William James, among others, commemorated his "martyrdom" in verse and prose.[10] The recent treatment of the story, however, highlights Shaw in a different way, using him as a medium for registering the pointed racial animus of the Union military, as his idealism seems to bring into the open the underside of white racial identity, its basis in racial exclusion and fear. In large part, the text divides its affirmative and critical messages regarding racial identity in such a way that the Shaw narrative becomes the locus of a critical interrogation of white identity, now disjoined from its usual central position. The story of the black troops, on the other hand, who had been marginalized to such a degree that the "Shaw Memorial" in Boston had originally been designed with no black soldiers represented, is made the positive focus of the narrative, which treats the sacrifices of the 54th as the genesis of a black narrative of American history.[11]

In many respects, *Glory* reverses the usual codes of racial representation, portraying white identity for much of the narrative in an expressly critical way, while representing the narrative of the black soldiers as a drama of origins, the tracing of a heroic lineage. But in other ways, the film recapitulates many of the traditional stereotypes of race. Whereas the character of Shaw is heavily psychologized in a manner that emphasizes his self-consciousness and awareness, the black soldiers are portrayed in a resolutely nonpsychological fashion, and are associated instead, as if by way of compensation, with a kind of spirituality and resilience. Additionally, the historical dimensions and traditions of white identity are stressed: Shaw's actual historical existence is underlined by specific references to his abolitionist family and to the political and military leaders of the day and through the use of his correspondence, rendered in the form of several first-person voice-overs scattered throughout the film. The black soldiers, on the other hand, are represented as bereft of historical tradition: the actual historical figures who served in the 54th, which included Frederick Douglass's two sons, are replaced by entirely fictional figures. Whereas the historical individuality of Shaw is underlined, the black soldiers are represented in the form of an ensemble of stereotypes in which the "Wild Tom," the "Uncle Tom," the "Buppie," and the rural hick are plainly represented.

Another striking difference in the way white identity and black identity are portrayed is in the dissimilar styles of language that characterize the two groups. In the voice-over that opens the text, for example, Shaw draws direct links among language, history, and national identity. Comparing the Civil War to the War of Independence, he says: "How grand it is to fight for the country, like the old fellows did in the Revolution. Only this time we must make it a whole country so that all can speak." The voice-over continues over images of life in the military camp and scenes of dispossessed blacks on the road, at which point we hear that the war is being fought "for a people whose poetry has not yet been written, but which will presently be as renowned and enviable as any." The character finishes the monologue with a quote from Emerson, whose words, he says, provide him with strength and comfort. These lines are typical of the discourse of the white officers. The refined speech of Shaw and his colleagues connotes class privilege, a sense of social obligation, and a long, stable, and unified tradition, one that assumes a perfect congruence of white racial identity and national identity.

In contrast to the unified tradition of Shaw, the black soldiers exhibit a range of dialects, verbal patterns, and rhetorical styles; the "poetry" to which Shaw alludes conveys a diverse sense of origins and a loose, patchwork form of connection. Thomas, for example, the eastern-educated black volunteer, must have the patois of a Sea Island black translated for him by another black soldier. Similarly, the exaggeration and deadpan humor of Trip proves incomprehensible to Jupiter, a rural black. Moreover, the motley regiment comes equipped with a mute drummer boy, whose practice and mastery of his instrument serves as a kind of synecdoche for the unit's growing sense of co-

hesion. Whereas Shaw's voice-overs, together with the speech patterns of the white officers in general, are clearly marked as "historical," the black soldiers' speech patterns are marked as geographically diffuse, underlining the film's strategy of treating the story of the 54th as a narrative of emergence.

One of the consequences of this strategy, however, is the elimination of all but the most glancing references to black participation in the established political and social traditions of the period. A case in point is the portrayal of Frederick Douglass, who is depicted at the beginning of the film in a way that promises to counterbalance the traditional emphasis accorded Lincoln in stories of the Civil War. Contrary to expectation, however, Douglass appears only in the company of the white establishment, and is never mentioned by the black soldiers, who appear to be wholly unfamiliar with him. This aspect of the film contradicts the view of historians who aver that Douglass was widely known and revered among the black population of the Civil War period. The bracketing of Douglass from the portrait the film offers is compounded by its overlooking the fact that Douglass's two sons, Lewis and Charles, served in the 54th, with Lewis becoming sergeant major. Moreover, the film fails to indicate that the first black Medal of Honor winner was a member of the 54th.[12] Although it tries to make racial struggle a "formative and necessary part of the story" of Ameri-

can history, to use the words of Nathan Huggins, the film provides only fictional "types" among the black soldiers, rather than the actual historical figures, whose presence would certainly lend its historical portrait a heightened degree of authority.[13] Another omission is the role played by the black intellectual Charlotte Forten, who worked as a teacher and nurse in the area where the 54th was encamped in South Carolina, and who had gained the admiration of Shaw. To some degree, the film treats the black soldiers and citizens of the period as bereft of historical tradition, understood in the conventional sense. The story of the 54th is instead constructed as the genesis, the mythic origin, of black historical consciousness.

But the history of black identity during the Civil War period that *Glory* suppresses with one hand it restores with the other; what Frederick Douglass called the "fleshly diploma" of slavery—the whip marks and other signs of physical abuse inflicted on the slave's or the ex-slave's body—comes to express another kind of tradition, another kind of history, one that functions in counterpoint to the dominant tradition.[14] Although the film erases much of the actual history of the 54th, it succeeds in creating a picture of a historical world that is shaped by radically different historical experiences, implying that there are potentially many histories embedded in a given historical moment. Moreover, the film suggests that black history and white history in the United States determine and shape one another. At certain points, it illuminates with surprising subtlety the deep, structural connections between the dominant tradition and the suppressed and marginalized history of racial domination, a theme that allows us to glimpse the outline of a more fundamental rewriting of the narrative of American history than we might have expected from this film, a rewriting that works against the convenient myth that, as Nathan Huggins puts it, "American history—its institutions, its values, its people—was one thing and that racial slavery and oppression were a different story."[15] By articulating these stories together, the film echoes the approach of historians such as Huggins, whose words could almost serve as an epigram to certain sequences: "Whereas the master narrative detached . . . slavery and the slave experience from the central story . . . there can be no white history or black history, nor can there be an integrated history which does not begin to comprehend that slavery and freedom, white and black, are joined at the hip."[16]

These ideas are powerfully expressed in the flogging scene in *Glory*, as Trip and Shaw reenact a historical pas de deux that suggests that the stories of white and black in America are inseparable and mutually defining. Trip, the black soldier whose defiant character has already called forth particularly intensive disciplinary procedures, has slipped out of camp to acquire some decent leather boots. Caught and assumed to be a deserter, Trip is brought before Shaw and the assembled company to be flogged. Shaw insists on this punishment, over the protests of his second in command, determined to show his control over the men as well as his control over his own emotions. As Trip is readied for the punishment, the drill sergeant pulls the shirt off of Trip's back to reveal a torso covered with scars from previous whippings. Despite his evident shock and dismay, Shaw sticks to the order he has given. As the whipping commences, however, a certain reversal takes place. In a series of close-up reverse shots, Trip's self-discipline and control over his body are underlined, as he receives the flogging without "breaking down." Shaw, on the other hand, appears to lose authority with each stroke of the whip, as his rigidity is coded not as a form of strength but as inflexible adherence to a code that has suddenly been revealed to have two different meanings, one having to do with military discipline, the other with racial domination.

The flogging scene in *Glory* departs from actual history—flogging was banned in the Union military—to make a larger point about the way the historical past marks black and white differently, but with the same pen. The whip marks on Trip's body are the signifiers of the other national narrative, a history that, although suppressed and marginalized, challenges the master narrative itself. Here, the film uses the imagery of scarred and lacerated flesh as a historical text to be read in counterpoint or, better, to be read interlinearly with the dominant narrative, like a coded message in which every other line carries the principal meaning, a meaning that often explicitly contradicts the text taken as a whole.

The commonality of these two histories is underlined by the physical mirroring of Trip and Shaw. Consider the following passage from Frantz Fanon on the way master and slave, colonizer and colonized, act out a kind of mirrored identification:

> A world divided into compartments, a motionless, Manichean world, a world of statues. . . . The first thing the native learns is to stay in his place and not go beyond certain limits. . . .
> . . . he finds he is in a state of permanent tension. . . . The symbols of social order—the police, the bugle calls in the barracks, military parades and waving flags—are at one and the same time inhibitory and stimulating: for they do not simply convey the message "Don't dare to budge"; rather they cry out "Get ready to attack." The impulse . . . implies the tonicity of the muscles. . . . The settler . . . keeps alive in the native an anger which he deprives of an outlet; the native [is] inwardly in a state of pseudopetrification.[17]

The flogging scene in *Glory* corresponds in an almost uncanny way to this description: the overall quality of motionlessness in its mise-en-scène, emblematized in the statuelike posture of Shaw versus the tensed, tight, muscular tonicity of Trip; the stiff formation of the soldiers; the trappings of military authority, the bugle call and drum roll, which evoke here the contradictory emotions that Fanon describes—"Don't dare to budge," as well as "Get ready to attack"— producing an adrenalized stasis that is plainly represented in the body postures of Trip, the soldiers, and Shaw himself. Although the "symbols of social order" clearly mean different things for blacks and whites, the effects of power position Trip and Shaw in similarly fixed and inflexible roles. In an instructive analysis of Fanon's imagery, Homi Bhabha points out that the play of polarities in his description of colonial relations—Subject/Object, Self/Other, Oppressor/Victim,

Power/Powerlessness—places both oppressor and victim in exceptionally similar predicaments: both are "pseudopetrified" in their antagonism.[18] In a similar fashion, Trip and Shaw become, in a sense, mirror
images; in Trip, a continuous physical tension marks the conflict between the proscriptions of social reality ("Don't dare to budge") and
the impulses of psychic reality ("Get ready to attack"), whereas in
Shaw, the immobilizing effects of authority seem to mummify the character, marking his features and his body posture with a kind of rictus
as he resolves to exercise the power of his office.[19]

Flogging scenes are a familiar staple of narratives set in the Civil
War period; what sets this sequence apart is its dialogic quality. Rather
than simply appealing to the masochistic or moral propensities of the
viewer, the sequence is explicitly staged as a challenge to the dominant
historical order and its way of perceiving race. Trip, a "graduate of the
peculiar institution with [his] diploma written on [his] back," to apply

the words of Frederick Douglass, has in effect "educated" Shaw about a history he had been insulated from, a history that transforms the punishment of Trip from the singular event that Shaw perceives it to be to the replaying of a historical pattern.[20] In a striking and pointed reversal, the scene suggests that it is Shaw's understanding of the historical past—and, by extension, white America's—that is mythological and folkloric. The dominant tradition, with its idealized conception of the American past, is itself a form of mythology insofar as it represses the history of race. As Huggins writes:

> The story of the United States is of the development of the North (read Puritan New England) rather than the South. It is of whites unrelated or unengaged with blacks. It is of freedom and free institutions rather than of slavery. It is as if one were to write a history of Russia without serious consideration of serfdom: a history of India ignoring caste. The distortion would be jarring did it not serve so well the national mythology and an idealized national character.[21]

Although the film appears at first to draw the most extreme contrast between the historicity of the white tradition and the folkloric nature of its version of black history, these terms end up being reversed, as one kind of historical knowledge confronts another.

Two Historical Trajectories

With the flogging scene, *Glory* produces a striking impression of "turning the tables" on the dominant tradition. But the overall thrust of the film—which is, I think, focused even more closely on white identity than on black—also channels the message of the sequence in another direction, bringing it back to the question of whiteness, to how the white hero will respond. The film uses this scene to instill in Shaw a layer of guilt that will be played on throughout the film. The linked themes of guilt, reparation, and reconciliation are from this point forward used to define the narrative of whiteness in a way that is distinct from the story of the black troops. Partly, this is a consequence of the psychologizing of Shaw, the focus on his emotions and sense of self-doubt. But it is also an aspect of the deeper fault line in the film, which configures the black narrative and white narrative along two different historical plotlines.

Like a painting with conflicting vanishing points, the film sets out different historical teleologies for blacks and whites. The narrative of collective emergence that characterizes the story of the African Americans is explicitly inverted in the story of Shaw, who we see discovering for the first time the hypocrisy of the white establishment. Continually confronted with venality, corruption, and lack of commitment in the military establishment, Shaw as a character becomes a way for the filmmaker to foreground the attenuation of the enlightenment narrative of history, of history unfolding in the service of liberty. With his continual wrestling with ethical dilemmas, and with the explicit message communicated through Shaw that the battle to be fought is not against an external enemy but rather against the internal complacency and self-interest of the whites, the Shaw narrative takes on the moral chiaroscuro more typical of the Vietnam film than the Civil War genre.

Nonetheless, Shaw is constructed as the hero of the narrative. Usually shown on horseback, often pictured in solitary contemplation of some distant horizon, Shaw is vested with the unmistakable iconography of the heroic. However, the film changes the meaning of his heroism from what it meant in the nineteenth century, for in *Glory* Shaw is constructed principally as a redemptive image of whiteness, a sacrificial figure who counteracts or "cleanses" the racial bias among the whites detailed throughout the film. Through Shaw, the narrative of whiteness becomes associated with social guilt and with the repayment of a historical debt. The theme of martyrdom, which dominated the Shaw legend in the nineteenth century, is here recoded to express a very different message of guilt and expiation.

In the scenes set on the road, the sense of a nation moving in two different historical directions is brought into relief. For example, one of the first shots in the film shows a mass of black families walking on the road near Antietam. As the film progresses, and as the soldiers of the 54th become increasingly disciplined and united in their resolve, the road is converted from an image of displaced drifting to a symbol of racial striving, with synchronized marching replacing images of wandering and admiring comments from bystanders supporting a sense of growing racial identity. One of the ways the film underlines the importance of the road motif is through its repeated use of close-up shots of running, marching, and bloodied feet. In a famous line, Frederick Douglass wrote, "My feet have been so cracked with the frost that the pen with which I am writing might be laid in the gashes."[22] The film reworks this image of wounded flesh, with its links to memory, into its own representational logic to signify the coalescence of a

historical force and the beginnings of a new historical epoch, as the march of the black troops through the South clearly evokes the civil rights marches of the 1960s. From this perspective, the film corresponds closely to Mikhail Bakhtin's description of the "novel of historical emergence," in which the hero "emerges along with the world and . . . reflects the historical emergence of the world itself." The soldiers of the 54th Infantry of *Glory* are represented "at the transition point between two historical epochs," a transition that is accomplished, to paraphrase Bakhtin, in them and through them.[23]

The motif of the road conveys a very different sense of historical meaning, however, when viewed in terms of the character of Colonel Shaw. Rather than an image of collective emergence, the road represents something like a religious *via crucis* for Shaw, one that stretches from his near brush with death at Antietam to his actual death at Fort Wagner. The construction of Shaw as a purificatory figure culminates in the scene on the beach immediately prior to the assault on Fort Wagner. Here, in a solemn moment of poetic introspection, Shaw is shown gazing out to sea, in the company of his horse. In this scene, marked by solitude, interiority, and a sense of an approaching "end," there is little suggestion of an impending social transformation on the horizon. Instead, Shaw becomes the locus of a critical, post-Vietnam-style interrogation of individual and collective morality, especially the morality of white America. The message of historical emergence associated with the black troops thus meets a sense of historical closure in the character of Shaw, as the film projects a dualistic image of nation, one in which scenarios of continuity or dissolution seem equally available as possible futures that might be generated from the events of the past.

Racial Identity into National Identity

In what is clearly the summit of the film's aspirations concerning the recovery of African American history, *Glory* provides a long, detailed treatment of the collective religious ceremony called the shout, in which the black soldiers of the 54th define their own sense of collective identity. The filmmaker, Edward Zwick, has said that discovering the "voice" for this sequence was particularly difficult, and that he relied on the black actors and their experience of contemporary churches to fashion it.[24] Here, the film shifts to a different rhetorical style and mode of address—Zwick claims that it was done in an almost improvisational way—to underline the black "authorship" of the scene. And despite Zwick's seeming disclaimer as to its historical authenticity, both the imagery and the call-and-response pattern of the shout accurately render the communal practices of black people during the Civil War years, including black Union soldiers preparing for battle.[25] Music and religion, as Paul Gilroy notes, were the two resources of communication and struggle available to slave cultures: "The struggle to overcome slavery, wherever it developed, involved adaptations of Christianity and politically infused music and dance, which, in Du Bois's phrase, comprised 'the articulate message of the slave to the world.'"[26]

But the significance of this scene lies less in its historical authenticity than in the way it opens to larger themes of racial and national identity, especially the translation of racial identity into national identity. The shout in many ways functions as a kind of nerve center of the text, bringing the issues of race and nation, of identity from below and identity from above, into vivid conjunction. As the camera focuses on the troops assembled around a campfire, a lead vocalist is seen singing lyrics that communicate a double message: the story of Noah's Ark as an allegory of the slave ship. Certain lines of the song make this relation explicit: "He packed in the animals two by two; / ox and camel and kangaroo; / He packed them in that Ark so tight / I couldn't get no sleep that night." The song underlines the themes of diaspora and wandering that will be played up throughout the sequence, and poetically converts the experience of slavery and displacement to a message of survival and providential guidance.

As the scene continues, the historical analogies encoded in song and testimony also continue, with each character's testimony accenting the themes of history and identity in a different way. Jupiter, for example, an illiterate field hand at the beginning of the film whose tutoring by the well-educated Thomas has been subtly insinuated into several scenes, speaks of going into battle with "the Good Book in one hand and the rifle in the other." The link between the Bible and the rifle calls to mind the particular accent black people of the period gave to the image of Jesus. As Lawrence Levine notes, Jesus was ubiquitous in the spirituals, but it was not the Prince of Peace of the New Testament that was celebrated but rather a Jesus transformed into an Old Testament warrior: "The God I serve is a man of war."[27] Jupiter's words also imply an image of a future that will be made with both the rifle and the book; the book, the film suggests here, is a weapon as powerful as the rifle and can serve as an agent of community, in this case bringing the rural field hand and the educated easterner together.

Another character, Rawlins, also makes a comparison to the Bible when he says that he has left his young ones and his kinfolk "in bondage." The phrase calls up images of the Israelites and the historical affinity of the black slave narrative with the story of Exodus. Finally, Trip gives a statement about the value of collective endeavor, couched in terms of family. Bereft of kin, continually on the run, Trip here redefines his tragic past through his identification with a larger collective endeavor. At the end of the sequence, Thomas, the cultured friend of Shaw, becomes the focus of the camera's attention. Although Thomas doesn't speak in this scene, he begins singing the chorus of the spiritual, clearly marking his identification with his fellow volunteers. As the film has progressed, Thomas has taken on an increasing understanding of a specifically black consciousness. When he is wounded in battle, for example, he vehemently insists that he "is not going back." The phrase conveys a double meaning. Not only does he refuse to be sent back to Boston and a life of comfort, "a cup of decent coffee, sitting by a warm fire, reading Hawthorne," as Shaw reminds him, but he refuses to go back to being a favored black man in an all-white culture. Thomas here seems to have fully embraced a black identity.

Stuart Hall has written of black identity as something that must

be constructed: "The fact is 'black' . . . has always been an unstable identity, psychically, culturally, and politically. It, too, is a narrative, a story, a history. Something constructed, told, spoken, not simply found. . . . Black is an identity that had to be learned and could only be learned in a certain moment."[28] The sequence of the shout strongly conveys this sense of identity being learned "in a certain moment"; black identity is "told" and narrated in such a way that a form of community emerges out of polyphony: a collective identity is here constructed from diverse voices and distinct trajectories. With Shaw manifestly excluded from the scene, the shout becomes a way for the potency and value of black collective life to pass directly to the spectator, as if the spectator were being invited to join in a dialogic ritual that, as Gilroy says, breaks down the division between spectator and performer. The signifiers of decline, isolation, and melancholy affixed to Shaw are directly countered by the vitality and exuberance of the black soldiers.

But as the film moves to its final, climatic scenes of battlefield carnage, this initial message of black identity as a dialectic of displacement and belonging is overlaid by the unifying paradigm of nationhood, in which the suicidal attack on Fort Wagner is configured as a necessary moment in the progressive unfolding of a plenary narrative characterized by racial and social advancement. In the ensuing scenes, the expressive form and language of the shout, which explicitly articulates a narrative of black diaspora, a narrative of dispersal, is placed in the service of a restored narrative of nation. Imagery that was used to express a fragmented, diaspora history is converted here to the expression of a coalescing nationalist sensibility. The variety of linguistic practices and the sense of geographic diffusion that have been associated with the black troops throughout the film are, in its closing scenes, renarrativized in terms of an exodus whose point of resolution is the nation-state. Although strong traces of African tradition can be found in the imagery and structure of the shout, the overall message that emerges is of a translation: vernacular black culture writing itself into, or being written into, the discourse of American nationalism.

The convergence of the theme of African American emergence with the theme of national identity is staged in a remarkably direct way. In the sequence that immediately follows the shout, the soldiers are depicted in tight, parallel formation, forming a corridor through which Shaw walks as he inspects the troops. After Shaw pauses to receive a Roman-style rifle salute from Jupiter, the film cuts to a high-angle close-up of the Stars and Stripes that literally fills the screen. Earlier, the symbolic meaning of "carrying the colors" had dominated a conversation between Trip and Shaw; Trip's refusal of this "honor" placed him on the far end of a continuum of identification and resistance that included Jupiter's eagerness to "wear the blue suits" and Rawlins's ambivalence about accepting the rank of sergeant major. But in the climactic attack on Fort Wagner, Trip has something like a battlefield conversion, seizing the colors and leading the charge, and immediately paying the price.

The "symbolic repertoire" of the community formed by the black soldiers has been portrayed in the film as relatively unfixed and still evolving, combining elements of Christianity, African tradition, local culture, and the codes of military life. But in the translation of this discontinuous history into a nationalist narrative, the film attempts to fix these symbols into universal meanings, capable of binding the whole "national community" together.[29] It attempts to assert, under the banner of the national, a sense of black and white "having a common story and necessarily sharing the same fate," an awareness of commonality that for Huggins, the author of this phrase, entails nothing less than a wholesale challenge and overturning of the master narrative of

American history.[30] *Glory* takes this ideal as its goal, but stops far short of Huggins's conclusions, tying identity, instead, all the more securely to identification with the nation-state.

In the final scene, in which Trip and Shaw are buried together in a mass grave along with the other dead troops, the film refers to Griffith's *Birth of a Nation* and its very different tableau of racial brotherhood—the dying embrace of two white soldiers fighting for opposing sides. Seen as a dialogic response to Griffith, *Glory* can be said to push the question of race back into history; rather than seeing the persistence of racism and the legacy of slavery as forces that complicate or diminish the central American story, *Glory* treats them instead as necessary parts of the story, a point that is underlined by the ominous ending of the film, in which the Confederate flag is shown being raised over the bodies of the defeated troops. The overall political and historical context of emancipation is dramatized, then, not from the perspective we might expect, not as a privileged moment of decisive social change in which black and white came together, but rather from the viewpoint of the present, with its awareness of the relapses, resistance, and reactions that continue to plague the course of the struggle for racial equality in this country.

For all of the ways that *Glory* could be said to challenge racist ideology, however, its most resonant appeal is to forms of nationalism that are themselves "colored with racial connotations," reinforcing some of the ideologies the film seeks to challenge.[31] Although it restores, to some degree, the historical dimensions of black life in the United States, it also refurbishes national symbols of authority that require the renunciation of cultural particularity. And the links the film establishes among patriotism, militarism, and nationalism, its endorsement of a "mystic nationhood" revealed only on the battlefield, reinforce the dominant fiction at the site of its greatest potential harm, where it can have the most lethal consequences. Nevertheless, in its interstices, the film retains a quality of skepticism about the power of what Raymond Williams calls the "artificial order" of the nation-state in comparison to the more complete order of "full social identities in their real diversity."[32] In its unusually direct examination of identity from across—the particularities of white and black identity defined in relation to one another—the film makes evident the limits of its own nationalist solution to racial difference and antagonism, projecting in

its closing images a message not about the end of slavery, but about the end of the nation as we know it. In the shots of the mass burial of the soldiers of the 54th that end the film, the national narrative is hauntingly evoked not as a triumphal story of social progress, but as a collective narrative of social loss.[33]

2 | Native America, *Thunderheart,* and the National Imaginary

Every state, according to Edward Spicer, is a plural entity, containing within itself two or more nations. Although the widespread use of the term *nation-state* tends to obscure the fact, the nation-state is not a "welded unity," but rather, almost without exception, consists of several entities that have long been considered nations in their own right, possessing distinct languages, histories, and cultural symbols.[1] Until recently, nation-states have generally succeeded in concealing or eradicating the cultural particularity of these "hidden nations"; today, however, partly due to the fascination of the mass media, many are becoming increasingly visible in ways that implicitly challenge the monological narrative of the state order. Native American nations are a striking case in point: historically among the most deeply hidden of the nations within the state, native nations have begun to break free of the "cocoon of invisibility" that the dominant culture had woven around them, an emergence thematized in several recent films that foreground the historical and poetic dimensions of native life.[2]

With this increasing visibility, Indian nations have also begun to acquire a different status and meaning within what Annette Hamilton calls the "national imaginary"—the collectively held images circulating within the dominant culture that aim to distinguish the "national self" from "national others."[3] In place of the disfiguring stereotypes of the past, Hollywood films and documentaries have recently visualized Indian nations as desirable alternatives to the nation-state, imaginative substitutes for a state order that, as one writer says, "has largely lost the ability to confer an adequate sense of identity upon its people."[4] Although Native Americans have yet to gain access to the resources to tell their own stories in feature-length films, the complex forms of identificatory desire evoked by works such as *Thunderheart, Geronimo, Pocahontas, Legends of the Fall,* and *Dances with Wolves,* along with recent documentaries such as *Five Hundred Nations* and *The Way West,* suggest that contemporary images of Native America have become even more powerfully imbricated with the national imaginary than in the past.

Hamilton employs the term *national imaginary* to describe the way cultural identity coalesces not simply around a set of positive images, but, just as important, in opposition to images of the other, against which the self, or the nation, can be distinguished. Rather than emerging from concrete experience, the national imaginary is formed from the circulation of negative images or stereotypes of national others against whom the national self is defined. Hamilton compares this oppositional logic with the Lacanian mirror-stage, "a moment in development when the child sees itself in the mirror, while thinking it sees another." Images of national "others," she argues, actually represent unacknowledged reflections or aspects of the national self: "Imaginary relations at the social, collective level can thus be seen as ourselves looking at ourselves while we think we are seeing others." Stereotypes of national others may be understood as the split-off parts of the national self, aspects of nation that are sensible or visible only when projected onto the other.[5]

The identities defining the national imaginary can change, however, when the nation's sense of coherence is threatened. Hamilton suggests that this is the case in Australia, where the need to secure a stable national image and identity, an identity that has never been adequately defined, has been exacerbated by the widespread influence of external cultural forms now inundating Australia as a consequence of globalization. This has led to a widespread reevaluation of what it is to be Australian, a reevaluation that has transformed the meaning and significance of the native Aboriginal culture for white society. Long seen as an undesirable internal other, Aborigines have recently acquired a new prestige as embodiments of an organic Australian culture and spirituality that has survived for thousands of years, an identity that the dominant culture now wishes to claim as an aspect of its own heritage. As Hamilton says, "Aboriginal identity may well become the Australian identity of the future, something not chosen by us, but imposed on us by the land itself."[6]

A similar shift appears to be occurring in the way Native Americans are perceived in the United States. Indians, of course, have long held a prominent position within the U.S. national imaginary, providing the principal terms of otherness—savagism, infantilism, cannibalism, madness—against which the nation-state has historically defined itself. Michael Rogin has shown how in the early years of U.S. settlement, the young nation's own insecurity and fear were projected onto the Indians, who became for the settlers imaginary embodiments of the infant stage of human evolution. Pictured as the "sons of the forest" or as "the children of nature"—images that dominated the political rhetoric of the 1800s—Indians were constructed both as symbols of a lost childhood bliss and "as bad children, repositories of murderous negative projections." The Indians "exemplified fears that the independent nation could not survive." They "attacked the young nation at its boundaries, keeping them confused and insecure . . . suggesting that early time when a secure self has not emerged, when it is threatened with retaliatory extermination for its own aggressive rage."[7]

In the present period, however, Native Americans have taken on another kind of meaning for the dominant culture. Figures of national imaginings for centuries, Indians have emerged in contemporary films as agents of a powerful counternarrative of nation, bearers of an alternative historical consciousness molded and shaped by centuries of incessant war, a message especially apparent in films such as *Thunderheart* and *Geronimo*. The theme of continuous struggle against the nation-state, a theme that defines many recent fiction films and documentaries on Native American life, can be seen as a crystallized and legitimate expression of the antagonism toward the nation-state that has become such a pervasive motif in contemporary American society, an antagonism Lauren Berlant describes as "refusing the interarticulation, now four hundred years old, between the United States and America, the nation and the Utopia."[8] The sense of ethnic mobilization and community characterizing the contemporary image of Native American nations conveys important lessons about the limits of the American national narrative and the changing character of national identity in the United States.

Thunderheart, a film directed by Michael Apted, provides a particu-

larly good illustration of the changing roles that Native American nations have assumed in contemporary national imaginings. In this chapter, I consider the film in light of two competing circuits of meaning
that I believe characterize the imaginary relation of the dominant culture to Native American nations today. I first examine the way the film
draws attention to the notion of Native American nations as the "first
nations" of North America, a concept that emphasizes the antiquity of
native cultures and the basis of Indian identity in the land. This idea is
powerfully expressed in the film's opening sequence, which fashions a
striking reversal of what might be called the "territorial imaginary" of
the nation-state, a reversal that calls into question the dominant metaphor of east-west "progress" and the basic model of history underpinning the master narrative of nation in the United States.[9] Second, I
note the way the film invites a kind of imaginary identification with
Native Americans, a tendency that the Indian writer Ward Churchill
says "empower[s] the non-native to begin to view him/herself as a new
hybrid, embodying the 'best of both worlds.'"[10] Although the contemporary fascination with the mystic space and spiritual power of native
North America filters into the film, its more vivid and resonant appeal
to identification derives from its refashioning of older national myths.
In its narrative patterning and visual design, *Thunderheart* draws substantially on what Mikhail Bakhtin calls the "genre memory" of the

western, one of the most enduring and important vehicles of national ideology in the United States.[11] The historical signals and cultural values associated with the western, what Hamilton calls "the relic imaginary of the past," interpenetrate and affect the construction of new images in *Thunderheart* in ways that suggest an affinity between the two nations, an affinity expressed in the narrative patterning of their primary war myths.[12] I will begin by analyzing the opening sequence of the film, which dramatizes in a highly condensed and symbolic form many of the themes and motifs discussed above.

Reversing the Territorial Imaginary

Thunderheart explores the particular circumstances and history of the Oglala Sioux, whose presence has been known to the dominant culture but whose cultural life has until recently remained largely invisible. Focalized through the perspective of an FBI agent who is selected to investigate a murder on the Pine Ridge Reservation because of his part-Indian ancestry, the film centers on the evolution of the main character as he comes to grips with his own partial and fragmented cultural identity. Underlining the ways nations survive within states—and stressing the persistence of Native American culture and identity in the face of continuing exploitation and domination—*Thunderheart* depicts the transformation of agent Ray Levoi, a seemingly mainstream American man, into an agent of the Lakota nation, a figure whose body, whose own DNA, comes to express a sense of internal otherness, of cultural alterity, and of a long-suppressed and competing concept of nationhood dwelling within the bordered imaginary of the nation-state.

One of the most striking ways the film distinguishes the Sioux nation from the nation-state that contains it is by contrasting the figures of temporality that serve to define their very different concepts of national belonging. Here I will enlist Benedict Anderson's influential description of the modern nation-state as an "imagined community," a description that stresses the link between national identity and the imagined parallelism and simultaneity of national life, emblematically figured in the structure of the newspaper and the realist novel, as a paradigm of the national order the film wishes to contest. Characterizing the modern nation as a kind of horizontal linkage of anonymous individuals moving along parallel pathways, Anderson argues that social cohesion is fostered and sustained mainly through the impression of temporal alignment promoted by the newspaper, the novel, the calen-

dar, and the clock—"a solid community moving steadily down (or up) in history." Simultaneity, in Anderson's view, is the principal trope of connection and belonging binding the disparate populations of the modern state together; the temporality of the modern nation, he writes, can be seen as forming a "complex gloss upon the word 'meanwhile.'"[13]

By contrast, *Thunderheart* emphasizes the sense of anteriority that molds and characterizes the identity of the Oglala Sioux, "a five-hundred-year connection: you can't break the thread," as one character says. The film's portrait of the Lakota nation is filled with references to and intimations of the past, with anteriority rather than simultaneity defining the tribe's principal form of social connection and national filiation. For the Oglala Sioux, national belonging is inseparable from an animistic conception of the world, characterized by spiritual experience and ancestral influences. Levoi, for example, is continually questioned about his kinship group as he conducts his investigation into the murder. Through a series of visions, he discovers that his grandfather was a powerful shaman who was killed in the massacre at Wounded Knee in 1890. The consciousness of nation that this produces in the main character, a consciousness of past tribulations rather than of past glory, creates a sense of agency that is very different from the attenuated forms of agency available to the citizen of the nation-state. Levoi, in epic fashion, saves his people from destruction by acting for the nation in a way that clearly fulfills a spiritual compact with the dead. The historical past is explicitly refigured here in terms of repetition and return, a theme that is literalized in Levoi's "vision" of being pursued at Wounded Knee, running among the "old ones," as if the history of the Oglala tribe were imprinted in the genetic memory of the main character.

These archaic and deeply sedimented ingredients of national identification are consistently contrasted with the "homogeneous, empty time" of the contemporary nation-state. Early in the film, when Levoi still identifies with the dominant culture, he is repeatedly shown checking his watch, "zapping" channels on his car radio, and working to meet an artificial deadline by which point the investigation must, ostensibly, be completed. As Fernand Braudel has pointed out, a "plurality of social times, a multiplicity of times" coexist in any given historical period.[14] *Thunderheart*, however, underlines the extent to which perspectives on time are intimately bound up with relations of power, a message that is expressed with exceptional precision in the opening sequence of the film.

In a scene that unfolds as a kind of time-lapse summary reminiscent of the opening reel of *2001: A Space Odyssey*, the film opens on a predawn landscape populated by Native American dancers circling a barren tree that has a few scraps of cloth attached to it. The symbolic repertory of the Lakota nation is immediately emphasized, as the silhouetted dancers are shown brandishing eagle feathers and wings; a staff with a crescent shape affixed to the end; a peace pipe, which is raised to the four cardinal directions, articulating the basic Lakota motif of a circle divided into four quadrants; and other artifacts. As the light of the rising sun encroaches on the sacred site, the dancers begin to fade from view and finally disappear. The camera then focuses on a lone Native American man, also seen in silhouette, running quickly uphill until gunshots ring out and blood and tissue explode from his chest, after which he plunges face down into a river. Moving along the surface of the water, the camera supplies a spatial transition as the color of the river changes, a modern bridge comes into view, and the sound of Bruce Springsteen's "Badlands" is heard on the sound track. The camera then rises to find the main character, Ray Levoi, driving a red Mustang on a Washington, D.C., freeway, impatiently switching channels on his car radio as he tries to negotiate a traffic jam. The sequence ends with a long shot of Washington, D.C., dominated by the shape of the Washington Monument, which forms a kind of visual rhyme with the sacred tree of the Native American dancers.

The iconographies of the two different nations are visualized here in terms that are expressly related to images of time; the crescent moon, the rising sun, the clockwise movements of the dancers, the symbolism of the four directions, which "coincide with temporal references to the four phases of human life," are explicitly opposed to what Anderson calls the "transverse, cross time" of the modern nation, conveyed through images of simultaneity and convergence, a "league of anonymous equals" drawn together by the broadcast band, the freeway system, and the clock.[15] The opening thus communicates a strong sense of what Bakhtin calls "heterochrony," the copresence of a multiplicity of social times, of competing histories and traditions that both overlap and diverge contained within the bordered territory of the United States.[16]

But temporal regimes also involve strategies of power and control, and in its reprise of the imagery of conquest—the "vanishing" dancers and the murder of a Native American man, who is seen fleeing in a westerly direction—the scene touches on the key historical metaphors of the dominant culture. These metaphors are encrypted into what one writer calls the privileged "east-west directionality of the hegemonic American master narrative," which condenses ideals of historical progress, racial hierarchy, and the expansion of the state.[17] As Roy Harvey Pearce writes, "The history of American civilization [is] conceived as three dimensional, progressing from past to present, from east to west, from lower to higher" (that is, from primitive to civilized).[18] Such "images of centrality," as Edward Said points out, typically undergird the master narratives of dominant societies, "embody[ing] certain sequences of cause and effect, while at the same time preventing the emergence of counter-narratives."[19] The narrative of progress, of an America stretching from sea to shining sea, thus depends precisely on the centrality of east-west images in the United States.

In *Thunderheart*, as in Leslie Marmon Silko's *Almanac of the Dead*, the overcoming of the dominant order is expressed as a shift in the directional and temporal axes that organize the plenary narrative of history in the United States.[20] The symbolic geography constructed in the opening scene can be read as reversing the territorial imaginary of the dominant culture; figures of space, time, and the hierarchy of "primitive" and "civilized" are invoked here in a way that communicates a certain remapping of the national paradigm of "progress." The causal and geographic link established between the reservation and Washington, D.C., a link that employs the symbolism of the river to connect the blood of the murdered Native American man to the capital and, by extension, to FBI agent Ray Levoi, whose own body will become a site of contestation between competing national orders, suggests that the dominant perspective here will be one that faces east.

As an imaginative restaging of events that occurred on and near the Pine Ridge Indian Reservation in the mid-1970s, *Thunderheart* dilates the historical and symbolic framework of the actual occurrences in order to create explicit links to the historical and mythic past, particularly to the epic story of Wounded Knee. As the film makes clear, the savage massacre at Wounded Knee in 1890 strengthened national identity and ethnic cohesion among the Sioux, furnishing an "epic legend on a grand scale"[21] that fostered a rebirth of national consciousness, most evident in the seventy-one-day siege at Wounded Knee almost one hundred years later, in 1973.[22] As Anthony Smith writes, "Ethnic consciousness [is] enhanced by adversity."[23] In many ways, *Thunderheart* centers on the way ethnic and national identity coalesces around the experience and memory of war. As the character Jimmy Looks Twice says, "It's a power deal . . . sometimes they have to kill us. They have to kill us, because they can't break our spirit . . . it's in our DNA. We know the difference between the illusion of freedom and the reality of freedom."

As a site of social memory, the Wounded Knee Monument plays an especially important role in the film. The main character, Levoi, visits the Wounded Knee Monument three times during the course of the film—first in the form of a vision of himself running with "the old ones," pursued by a mounted soldier who seems to emerge from the shadow of the monument itself. This vision is followed by a second, actual visit in which Levoi checks for the name of his ancestor, Thunderheart, on the grave stela. Finally, at the end of the film, Levoi visits the grave of the activist leader Maggie Eagle Bear, who was murdered because she discovered the illegal uranium drilling taking place on Indian lands.

At another level, however, the film appears to rely on a different national mythology, the genre of the western, to shape a new war myth with Native Americans as protagonists. Employing many of the visual tropes and narrative conventions of the western, *Thunderheart* prizes

out and critiques many of the ideological and racial messages embedded within the form, but it also rehearses a narrative pattern that forms part of the substratum of national mythology in the United States. In *Thunderheart*, a solitary hero, an outsider, acquires a sidekick and acts for the collective in a way that ensures the future of the community, only to ride off alone into an uncertain future at the end. By engaging the genre memory of the western as a war myth, a war myth that can be transposed and reenacted from the perspective of the margins, the film offers a kind of mythic continuity of identity between the two nations that would otherwise be lacking.

The Western and the National Imaginary

The Cherokee artist and writer Jimmie Durham has said that "the negation of Indians informs every aspect of American culture. . . .

America's narrative about itself centers upon, has its operational center in, a hidden text concerning its relationship with American Indians. That central text must be hidden, sublimated, acted out." Although many aspects of the American myth are now being critically examined, he writes, "the central, operational part, the part involving conquest and genocide, remains sacred and consequently obscured. . . . The indigenous populations must be always and essentially unreal, a figment of the national imagination."[24]

One of the most durable and effective masks for this disguised operational center of the nation-state has been the western, a genre that has furnished much of the basic repertoire of national mythology for the United States throughout the twentieth century. As a form that preserves older concepts of nation while illuminating present-day conflicts and concerns, the western stands as an especially good illustration of Bakhtin's concept of "genre memory." Genres function, Bakhtin writes, as "organs of memory" for particular cultures, providing crystallized forms of social and cultural perception that embody the worldviews of the periods in which they originated, while carrying with them "the layered record of their changing use." Genres "remember the past [and] redefine present experience in an additional way." A genre form such as the western offers a vivid realization of this concept, for it clearly functions as a "repository of social experience" that preserves certain historical perspectives even as it has been adapted to new contexts.[25]

As a myth of national origins, the western serves an emblematic nationalist function, for it is a form capable of mediating and containing the central contradiction in American ideology—the contradiction posed by race. Although national identity in the United States is traditionally conceived as a "deep, horizontal comradeship," an "imagined community" of equals characterized by "social unisonance," the actuality of racial hierarchy and oppression and the drive for dominance by certain groups starkly contradicts this idealized image. In a recent essay, Virginia Wright Wexman argues that the imagery of the frontier— understood as a line of demarcation between civilization and the wilderness—and the myth of westward expansion at the heart of the western genre are exceptionally useful vehicles of legitimation for the nation-state, for they serve to justify the appropriation of Indian lands and the domination of racial others: "What is most conspicuously at issue in Westerns is . . . the right to possess the land. . . . Both the genre and the images of its major stars . . . define land in terms of property and cultural dominance in terms of racial privilege."[26]

Thunderheart opens a kind of dialogue with the tradition of the western, offering a subtle analysis of the interlocking myths of the American empire while also, at particular points, claiming certain of these myths for its own purposes. Drawing on the western's principal visual and narrative strategies, the film effectively exposes links between images of landscape and the domination of indigenous people, between the vision of a community carved from the wilderness and the reality of conquest and colonial occupation, between the myth of settler heroism and the continuing reality of native resistance. From this perspective, the film can be seen as a kind of counterwestern, exposing the five-hundred-year-old struggle over land and the genocide that accompanied it as the concealed basis of the myth of the frontier and the epic narrative of westward expansion.

From another perspective, however, *Thunderheart* appears to embrace the imaginary it seeks to contest, depicting the ancient collectivity of the Lakota people in ways that seem to rehearse the western paradigms that the film strives to counteract. For example, the film depicts a Native American community that has been shaped by conflict and adversity, whose ethnic cohesion and identity have been molded by a continuous state of war. Now warfare, as we know from Anthony Smith, is one of the chief forces shaping ethnic cohesion and identity; prolonged warfare especially, he argues, promotes and strengthens ethnic self-consciousness and ethnic imagery: "Societies . . . owe much of their form and solidarity to the exigencies of war. . . . it is external conflict which shapes ethnic community, and more especially, its images."[27] *Thunderheart*'s use of the conventions of the western, which might be called the principal war myth of the American nation-state, to reinforce the image of martial solidarity it ascribes to the Indians is a striking example of the national imaginary at work—"ourselves looking at ourselves while we think we are seeing others." Rather than fixing on the "mystic space and spiritual power" of native North America, the film suggests that it is the image of a nation at war that best captures the "mythological and spiritual continuity of identity" that the dominant culture desires.[28] What I would like to stress in this part of my analysis is the way *Thunderheart* engages the tropes of the western in order to expose the theme of racial dominance as the "operational center" of the western myth, while at the same time appropri-

ating key aspects of this genre form in order to symbolize Native American identity in a way that fulfills the self-image of the dominant culture.

The Western and Its Tropes of Space and Nation

As a dramatic locale for myths of origins, the western landscape has often been associated with what the Australian critic Ross Gibson calls a "cornucopic mythology," a mythology symbolized by the passage from allegorical desert to garden in the storied settling of the West. Rather than being seen as a "thoroughly edited text, that already contains lessons for survival," the western landscape is instead viewed as a pristine surface receptive to the imprint of civilization, progress, and settlement.[29] Dramatic images of landscape are, of course, one of the chief generic markers of the western, which often features plots revolving around struggles over land. Even where land is not at issue, as Wexman points out, westerns invariably refer to its centrality by setting a great number of scenes against imposing natural landscapes. Panoramic shots emphasizing the scale and the emptiness of western landscapes are important signifiers of national mythology, for they suggest not only the grandeur of nature but also a kind of open potentiality: "Westerns often dwell on wordless images of the landscape. . . . the landscape is rendered as an object of discovery by the seer, who is

placed in a position of dominance. . . . Seemingly limitless views function as a prelude to the imperialist mission of defining territories and
scanning perimeters. . . . The landscape's provocative emptiness invites
the spectators imaginatively to penetrate and possess it."[30]

Thunderheart treats the landscape, however, as a window onto
the genocidal past; the panoramic landscape shot is evoked in order
that it may be critically examined. At several points in the film, the
camera glides at a high angle over the terrain of the Badlands in a kind
of accelerated tracking shot, both recalling the western convention of
high-angle panoramas—described by Wexman as the "master of all I
survey" scene—and disclosing what might be called the political unconscious of the unbounded western vista. Early in the film, for example, the camera abruptly descends from the lush greenery of the plain
to a desertic crevice, a huge crack in the earth, to reveal the rotting
corpse of a Native American man, face down in the dirt. A shot that
began as a lyrical quotation of the myth of the virgin lands concludes
with a dead Indian dominating the frame, and with the offscreen
voices of approaching FBI agents claiming "jurisdiction" over the
body. Far from revealing the "placid movements of horses, wagon-
trains, or cattle being driven to market," or from inviting spectators
to "imaginatively penetrate and possess it," the landscape here is
coded as a site of political and racial struggle.[31] The film effectively revises the scenic interlude of the landscape shot in such a way that the
history of racial and cultural domination sedimented within it is
brought to the fore.

From the opening scene of the vanishing ghost dancers through the
vision that Ray Levoi experiences of running with the "old ones" at
the first massacre of Wounded Knee, the landscape presents itself as a
historical text—not as an object to be subdued or as something preter-
natural and sublime, but rather as "something to be learned from."[32]
The lessons the landscape teaches in *Thunderheart*, however, are not
so much the ecological lessons associated with Native American land-
culture—although the plundering of Indian lands for uranium ore is
a central element of the film's investigative plot—but rather the historical lessons that define and reinforce Indian imagery and identity.
Here the historical past—specifically, the memory of the massacre at
Wounded Knee—imbues the landscape with meanings very different
from those conveyed by the narrative of the nation-state.

One of the key ways the film expresses this idea is by resuming the

century-old narrative of Wounded Knee in the frame of the present. Here, the film literally restages the flight of the Indians toward the "stronghold," a kind of natural fortress in the rock cliffs near Wounded Knee. In 1890, the Indians never reached the stronghold and were massacred by an overwhelming federal force. In *Thunderheart*'s climactic scene, however, the two main Indian characters make it to the base of the stronghold, where the assembled Lakota people confront the pursuing federal officers and rescue Levoi, whose ancestor, "Thunderheart," was killed while running to this natural fortress nearly a century before.

The legends that are embedded in this landscape, then, are the legends of the Native American people. Even the nomenclature of the land—the stronghold, the source, the monument, the Knee—communicate a sense of space that is imbued with potent national imaginings. Landscape in *Thunderheart* is invested with a narrative and symbolic dimension that consolidates and inspires native collective identity, rather than settler identity, and that propels it in the direction of nation formation.

War and the Forging of Ethnic Community

The imagery of war that so effectively links contemporary Indian struggles to the tribulations of the past also seems to echo the very nationalistic myths that the film seeks to overturn. The climactic standoff at the stronghold, for example, which appears to rewrite the massacre at Wounded Knee in order to change its outcome in the present, can also be seen as a borrowing from the western. From this perspective, the theme of Indian resistance appears to be laminated to the visual and narrative conventions of the western in ways that solicit an imaginary continuity of identity between the dominant culture and Indian nations.

Although the dramatis personae of the classic shoot-out are reversed, echoes of the western reverberate through this scene. After the Native American heroes have been chased through the desert landscape, they arrive at the base of the stronghold, where Levoi, who has now become an ally of the traditional Indians he initially opposed, faces off against his former mentor, Frank Coutelle—a scene that explicitly rehearses the classic western showdown. Levoi and his sidekick, Crow Horse, however, decide not to shoot it out, and turn their backs on Coutelle and his assembled gunmen to begin walking toward the stronghold. At this point, it appears that they will be shot from behind in precisely the same fashion their ancestors were in the first massacre at Wounded Knee. Just as Coutelle raises his gun, however, a large company of traditional Indians appear at the top of the fortress-like cliff, with rifles trained on the villains below. The FBI agent Coutelle wheels with his rifle in several different directions and, seeing himself surrounded, retreats. The camera then tracks up and away to reveal the deployment of traditional Indians in the stronghold, a deployment that suggests and recalls countless images of soldiers and settlers in westerns defending their outposts and forts against Indian attack.

The standoff at the stronghold dramatizes an instance of collective mobilization that seems to revitalize the Lakota nation, activating the latent energies of the people who had been depicted throughout as essentially passive. But in depicting the mobilization of the Lakota people in a manner that so clearly echoes the western formula, *Thunderheart* encourages an imaginary identification with the Indians on the part of the dominant culture. Moreover, the scene at the stronghold depicts the entire population of traditional Indians, including grandmothers and Grandpa Reaches, the holy man, defending their nation, creating a powerful image of national cohesion. Here, the image of the Indian other serves quite clearly as an image of an idealized national self, a national self that apparently requires "the hammer of incessant war" to beat it into national shape, and that must now look to the other for images of social coherence.[33]

Nevertheless, one could also argue that the film's use of the western to create a potent, militant image of the Lakota Sioux represents a sifting of the form, rather than a wholesale reproduction. *Thunderheart* retains certain aspects of the western genre while repudiating others, emphasizing the mobilization of the Lakota people as a means of survival, not as a strategy of conquest. Rather than expressing a competitive, acquisitive attitude toward land, or expressing a myth of spiritually sanctifying violence, as in the mythology of "regeneration through violence" that Richard Slotkin finds at the heart of American ideology, *Thunderheart* addresses the western as a myth of collective survival, retaining its imagery of ethnic cohesion while repudiating its conquistadorial message concerning the land.[34] Thus, the film draws on the conventions of the western but imbues them, as Bakhtin might say, with a very different "social accent."[35]

Conclusion

By emphasizing the fact that the state's campaign of conquest and genocide continues in the present and that Indian resistance is ongoing, *Thunderheart* constructs a frame of encounter that conflicts with the narrative of the nation-state as a "continuous, homogeneous subject."[36] It echoes the activist view that "the Indian wars have never ended in America," employing the imagery of war in ways that reinforce crucial aspects of Indian identity and nationhood. This powerful evocation of Indian solidarity may also be seen, however, as a projection on the part of the dominant culture. As identification with the nation-state continues to wane in the absence of what Smith calls the "hammer of incessant war"—an essential condition, it appears, of social cohesion and strong self-images—Native American nations have begun to assume a heightened importance in the national imaginary as emblems of solidarity and self-determination. Resituated in the master American narrative as embodiments of desirable cultural values—above all, the values associated with the image of the warrior—Native Americans are now being appropriated as cultural progenitors, as American ancestors, "the first and best blood of America," as one writer calls them, whose most exemplary characteristics can be imagined as a form of cultural inheritance.[37]

But in a period when armed militias have declared war on the

American nation-state and have begun to construct their own myth-
ologies around Waco, the deaths of Randy Weaver's wife and son, and
the bombing of the Federal Building in Oklahoma City, it is important
to distinguish the militant self-image of the "first nations" of the
Americas from those of militias founded on ideological beliefs. Native
American art, music, and spirituality speak to the organic and authentic nature of Indian culture; the social mobilization in defense of their
nations that characterizes Native Americans' activism is a clear response
to their actual conditions of existence. Where *Thunderheart*'s depiction of the Lakota nation clearly departs from other recent manifestations of ethnic nationalism, both within and outside the United States,
is in the absence of a sense of "ideological destiny," of abstract ideals
and territorial aspirations. The pursuit of a political ideal supported by
an institutional, ideological program that animates the militia movement, as well as many other ascendant nationalisms, is a characteristic

that gives them a striking similarity to the nation-state order they ostensibly contest. *Thunderheart*, in contrast, stresses the ancient cultural reality of the Lakota people, which it depicts as largely free of concepts of destiny, ideology, or abstract political aspirations. Perhaps the strongest lesson the film has to offer is that nations do not need to become like states to promote the historical consciousness essential to the formation of community.

3 | National Identity, Gender Identity, and the Rescue Fantasy in *Born on the Fourth of July*

Born on the Fourth of July can be read as a particularly complex variant of the cultural tendency that Susan Jeffords has called "the remasculinization of America": the restoration of patriarchal concepts of nation through narratives that emphasize the renewal of masculine identity in the post-Vietnam period.[1] Whereas Oliver Stone's film pointedly criticizes traditional myths of masculinity based on concepts of "punitive agency," it nevertheless asserts the importance of the masculine role in a changing narrative of nation. Linking the iconography of nationalism to the symbolism of gender in an overt way, the film anatomizes the failure of masculinist national ideals in the Vietnam period, offering in its closing scenes an alternative image of nation based on the metaphor of a maternal, social body America, an "America who can embrace all her children."[2] But despite the film's attempt to revise the gender dynamic of national identity, the metaphor of nation as woman in *Born on the Fourth of July* serves mainly to set the scene for a narrative in which the male hero gains authority by "rescuing" the nation from its own weakness, a pattern that closely resembles the unconscious fantasy that Freud calls the "rescue motif."[3] Whereas the film defines the role of the male hero in ways that suggest alternative approaches to masculine identity, its symbolic structure, organized around a series of maternal stereotypes, reveals a deep gender ambivalence. Its metaphors for nation range from maternal love (the nation as "milk-giver") to the nation as "blood-seeker" (a vampire), as if the film's uncertainty toward its own nationalist agenda were projected onto the female figures in the text.[4] In *Born on the Fourth of July*—the film's title underscores the dominance of the metaphor—maternal images are elevated into emblems of national cohesion on one side or degraded to images of perversion and division on the other.

In its symbolic and metaphoric trajectory, the film thus appears to confirm Jeffords's thesis that by reaffirming masculinity, the Vietnam narrative also reaffirms other relations of dominance, particularly those of patriarchy. Indeed, this view constitutes the currently accepted critical perspective on the Vietnam film, a perspective that also discerns a straightforward oedipal patterning as the basis of the drama of masculine subjectivity in these films.[5] But *Born on the Fourth of July* also departs from Jeffords's description of the "masculine frame of narration" in significant ways as well, particularly in its equation of what Laura Mulvey has called "the overvaluation of virility under patriarchy" and the social problems of the Vietnam era.[6] Casting the protagonist as a victim of patriarchal society, the film draws on the generic resources of melodrama, a genre long associated with feminine emotion, to articulate the gap between masculinist cultural ideals and the lived experience of the protagonist. Moreover, whereas the suppression and subordination of the feminine serves, in the view of many critics, as the fulcrum of masculine renewal in Vietnam films, *Born on the Fourth of July* links the recovery of the male hero to the rescue scenario, with its emotions of "gratitude," "love," and "tenderness," and to the substitution of a feminine ideal of national identity for the fracturing violence of patriarchal concepts of nation.[7] In its portrait of the Vietnam veteran as victim of patriarchy on the one hand and as rescuer of a nation imaged as feminine on the other, the film solicits a more complex reading of masculine agency in the Vietnam film than has been given to date.[8]

Jeffords argues that narratives about Vietnam are most deeply concerned with the restabilizing of gender roles, that gender is what representations of the Vietnam era are about: "Though Vietnam representation displays multiply diverse topics for its narratives and imagery, gender is its determining subject and structure. . . . Gender is the matrix through which Vietnam is read, interpreted and reframed in dominant American culture."[9] Despite the Vietnam narrative's characteristically critical perspective—its display of the "apparent dissolution of traditional forms of power"—it functions largely, in Jeffords's understanding, to reinforce the authority of the state: "Along with the re-negotiation of masculinity has come a renegotiation and reempower-ment of the state. . . . rather than the Vietnam experience challenging the current structures of American society, it seems only to enhance them."[10] In contrast to Jeffords, I believe that *Born on the Fourth of July*, which I take as an emblematic Vietnam film and one most di-rectly concerned with the project of remasculinization, presents a highly critical view of the close relation between masculine identity and na-tionally sanctioned aggression. To a large extent, the generic codes of melodrama that structure this film conflict directly with what Jeffords calls the "masculine point of view." Rather than expressing the "inter-ests, values, and projects of patriarchy," the film employs melodrama in order to present a historical critique and counternarrative of Ameri-can identity conceived along masculinist lines.[11] At the same time, how-ever, the film finally conveys through its melodramatic structure a model of national community based on the nuclear family, to some degree reaffirming traditional forms of gender identity as the dominant per-spective through which national identity is realized. *Born on the Fourth of July* can thus be seen as an exemplary manifestation of the complex nature of the Vietnam narrative, in which the most significant issues of national identity, gender identity, and the narrative forms that convey and reinforce them are set into new and shifting configurations.

In the pages that follow, I examine the film in terms of three closely related strategies of representation. I begin by delineating the film's use of melodramatic conventions and structures, which serve as an index of its social ideology and which contrast with the forms of narrative that Jeffords associates with the project of "remasculiniza-tion." Second, I consider the film's analysis of masculine identity and argue that the film puts particular pressure on the link between mas-culinity and punitive concepts of historical agency. Third, I discuss the film's use of maternal metaphors of nation to demonstrate that its ideal-ized image of a maternal, social body America departs from masculin-ist ideology while at the same time allowing the film to represent the hero as a paternal figure, as the "rescuer" of the nation, restoring the myth of the nuclear family as an emblem of promised community. I begin by discussing the film's use of the genre codes of melodrama, which convey a set of messages that both complicate and extend the "masculine frame of narration" that Jeffords argues prevails in Viet-nam representations.

Melodrama and National Identity

The historical signals emitted by particular genre forms constitute an important part of the messages we receive from individual texts. As Mikhail Bakhtin argues, genres impose their own historical perspectives and systems of value on a work, both recalling past usages and illuminating the present in new ways. In the Vietnam film, critics and theorists have, for the most part, sidestepped the issue of genre by, on the one hand, claiming that the Vietnam film constitutes a genre in its own right or, on the other, stressing the Vietnam narrative's oedipal configurations and its conversion of political and ideological issues into scenes of technospectacle.[12] In my view, however, the genre patterning of the Vietnam film, which can generally be characterized as melodramatic, constitutes a rich source of critical insights, allowing us to link the Vietnam narrative with earlier cultural attempts to come to grips with national trauma.

Melodrama has often functioned as an important vehicle of popular historical interest, and has, in times of crisis, helped to mold and influence concepts of national identity. In the view of George Lipsitz, melodrama constitutes a privileged form of popular connection with the past, and has provided a "particularly significant form of participation and investment within American commercial culture since World War II."[13] David Grimstead traces the influence of melodrama on national consciousness back to the nineteenth century, when theatrical melodrama played an important role in defining the national narrative. According to Grimstead, melodrama served as the "echo of the historically voiceless." Its stress on direct feeling as an index of moral value functioned, he maintains, as a "'great equalizer,' bypassing inequalities of class and education," and providing a source of national identity for a country convinced of the radically egalitarian nature of its social experiment.[14] Frank Rahill similarly attributes the rise of American melodrama to the need to redefine national identity after the Civil War. The cycle of "frontier sagas" and Civil War dramas that dominated the American stage in the 1880s provided "the sought for national drama."[15] In short, melodrama has served in the past as a way of framing U.S. national identity in terms of democratic and egalitarian ideals.

In the Vietnam narrative, melodrama has again assumed a privileged role in the articulation of national identity, but in a way that is different from its function in the nineteenth century. As exemplified by *Born on the Fourth of July*, the genre conveys certain historical signals and a consistent system of values, but it has acquired a different "social accent" as it confronts a new context.[16] In making this comparison, I wish mainly to underline the ways that genres function, as Bakhtin says, as forms of cultural memory. Genres are best understood, he argues, as repositories of social experience, crystallized forms of social and cultural perception, "organs of memory" that embody the worldviews of the periods in which they originated, while also carrying with them the "layered record of their changing use."[17] In his view, they are the principal vehicles for shaping and carrying social experience from one generation to another, the connecting "'drive belts from the history of society to the history of language' and literature."[18] Through the process Bakhtin calls "genre memory," aesthetic forms both "remember the past . . . and redefine present experience in an additional way."[19] This leads to the concept of "double-voicing," which occurs when an older genre is adapted to a new context.

In *Born on the Fourth of July*, melodrama retains its historical provenance, visible in its emphasis on the claims of emotion and in its attempt to frame national identity in terms of familial relations.[20] More important, however, it defines the Vietnam narrative in a way that allows it to be joined to the broader national narrative, imposing a kind of teleological resolution on a national trauma whose materialization in culture has been exceptionally partial, protracted, and resistant to completion. The structural patterns of melodrama serve to fill out and set into place a narrative project—the cultural narrative of the Vietnam War and its aftermath—whose symbolic resolutions have only slowly seeped to the surface. The essential character roles and narrative patterns of the Vietnam "experience" congeal in *Born on the Fourth of July* into a form in which the historical period now appears to be rounded out and resolved, translated from the realm of political and ideological contradiction to the realm of universal family values. This is accomplished in the film through the use of the generic patterns of melodrama in both critical and affirmative ways, to critique the role of the family for its complicity in the war and yet to reaffirm the cultural role of the Vietnam veteran as rescuer of the nation and as paternal figure, the begetter of a new national paradigm.

In the film, which I see as both a compendium of Vietnam themes and the culminating work of the cycle, the theme of victimization is ac-

companied by two additional melodramatic tropes that can be isolated as fundamental to the historical project of the film: the trope of "misrecognition" and the device of the "rescue." The trope of misrecognition dominates the first half of the film, bringing the Janus-faced nature of national identity into relief as the seemingly irreconcilable gulf between the ideals of the protagonist and the actuality he confronts, between his past and his present, opens up a series of contradictions. The rescue motif organizes the second half of the film, allowing the male protagonist to redeem himself by "saving" the nation and restoring the national community to a form more closely resembling the ideal American homeland, a motif that is facilitated by the metaphoric identity of nation and woman.

By first approaching *Born on the Fourth of July* from this perspective, I wish to show how the film utilizes the cultural memory embedded in genre to shape and define its historical message. The "remasculinizing" narrative trajectory of the film is both qualified and reinforced by this generic intertext. In addition to misrecognition and the rescue motif, many of the most typical melodramatic tropes and devices are used in the film as forms of critical analysis: betrayal, villainy, victimization, and the personification of social forces in emblematic characters are recoded to express the rejection of older ideologies and the formulation of a different form of national identity.

Throughout the first half of the film, the main character, Ron

Kovic, enthusiastically presents himself as the representative of a nationalistic tradition defined by military force and moral rectitude. But after participating in the massacre of women and children in a Vietnamese village, witnessing the cover-up of his own accidental killing of another American soldier, and then being severely wounded himself, the character is wrenched from his secure historical identity and experiences a kind of dissolution of self. Paralyzed from the chest down, he sees himself as a victim of all the institutions that had previously defined him: family, community, the armed forces, history itself. The film uses his estrangement from the past to explore the erosion of a historical order that had imprinted itself on the gestures, behavior, and attitudes of his social milieu.

The first part of the film in many ways echoes the tendency Christine Gledhill describes in her discussion of King Vidor's *The Crowd*: "A specific date links a national historical occasion with an individual birth rather than a social fabric. . . . The nation's story will be vested in the individual trajectory."[21] Emphasizing both the typicality and the "individuality" of the main character, the opening scenes of the film unfold as a kind of diorama of national stereotypes: young Kovic playing "soldiers" and baseball, celebrating his birthday at a Fourth of July parade, being kissed by a girl to the accompaniment of fireworks, competing in high school athletics. The common identity of nation and individual is evoked and underlined through the exceptional typicality of these scenes. But the "uniqueness" of the character is also asserted, most directly by Kovic's mother, who calls her son her "Yankee Doodle Dandy" and who singles him out by relating her premonitory dream, on the occasion of President Kennedy's inauguration, that Ron will one day be speaking in front of a large crowd.

By presenting these scenes in a visual style that is almost operatic—moving from one dramatic set piece to another, with few of the connecting devices of narrative, with slow motion and music augmenting their emotional temperature—the film expresses both a sense of intense feeling and a sense of falseness and inauthenticity. The small-town world of the 1950s and early 1960s is portrayed in the opening in an overtly nostalgic manner that is strikingly reminiscent of the "Morning in America" theme of Ronald Reagan's presidential campaign. The hometown universe of the protagonist is shown to be thoroughly permeated by the mythology of the period: pop songs, the

Kennedys, Marilyn, the Yankees, television, family, the memory of World War II. These leitmotivs of mid-twentieth-century America encapsulate a world steeped in popular legend, a world replete with mass-produced images through which characters live out their lives. In foregrounding these stereotypes of the fifties and early sixties, the film emphasizes the consensual nature of the society, the cocoonlike enclosure of a period in which the dominant culture was largely unchallenged. Although the cultural changes associated with the youth movement and the civil rights movement were certainly apparent by 1965, ideological conflict is almost entirely absent from the suburban world the film depicts. Instead, the film emphasizes the naïveté and emotional idealism of the dominant culture of the early sixties, the contentment and complacency that Fredric Jameson calls the "misery of happiness," the self-satisfaction of small-town life that is seen to represent the whole of pre-Vietnam America.[22] The overall strategy of the film, however, is not so much to repudiate this picture of national life, which will be resurrected in the closing moments of the film, as to revise it and transfer its authority to more progressive features of the national text.

The second major sequence of the film functions as an explicit reversal of the opening boyhood scenes. After being wounded in Vietnam, Kovic is sent to a Veterans Administration hospital to recover from his paralyzing injury. With its scenes of physical deterioration, body wastes, and psychological degradation, the hospital sequence at-

tains the status of Grand Guignol without departing from a realistic portrait of the milieu. Rats, physical abuse, a negligent medical staff, the omnipresence of death and putrefaction—all are conveyed in a urine-yellow color and in a series of shock cuts that contrast vividly with the filtered luminescence of the boyhood scenes. In the contrast between the sentimentality and emotionalism of the opening and the historical and personal tragedy of Vietnam, the film insists upon the radical alterity of the two experiences, but it also implies a necessary connection between the two. The stark antitheses distinguishing the boyhood sequences and the body of the film function as a kind of dramatic reversal, which Thomas Elsaesser claims often has the effect of "exposing the incurably naive moral and emotional idealism in the American psyche." Elsaesser argues that melodrama uses sentiment and emotion in a dialectical way: by identifying characters with illusory hopes and self-delusion, and then forcing a confrontation "when it is most wounding and contradictory,"[23] melodrama opens up contradictions that realism, by contrast, seeks to contain.[24]

In scenes reminiscent of the crusading melodramas of Dickens, Hugo, and Eugène Sue, the film's indictment of government institutions and politics is set out in the language of individual victimage. Its withering critique of the V.A. hospital system, which can be taken as emblematic of larger social pathologies, is centered on the private ordeal of Ron Kovic, continuously processed through the subjective experiences of the protagonist. Sequences of physical and psychological distress are intercalated, however, with Kovic's initial encounters with black consciousness and with the antiwar movement to suggest a dawning awareness of a larger social pathology, a social system in an extreme state of unhealth, rendered in microcosm in the world of the V.A. hospital. These themes can be glimpsed in a dream sequence in which Kovic rises from his bed and walks past his gray, unconscious roommates, fellow victims of institutional neglect, who seem to come to life as he passes—a sequence that foreshadows his later political role. But in the closed world of the V.A. hospital, he cannot shape events or influence his milieu: he is acted upon. He becomes a typical protagonist of melodrama, acquiring what Elsaesser calls a "negative identity through suffering."[25]

In the course of these two antithetical scenes, the film plays heavily on the melodramatic device of misrecognition. Kovic, the film implies, has misrecognized the true nature of the nation, and he is now being confronted with the reality of national life. Thrust from a childhood world of glistening surfaces to a world of Goyaesque disasters, he is unable to recognize himself, or the America that he left behind; the fixed points of his ideological compass simply do not correspond to the reality he encounters. The theme of misrecognition is articulated to greatest effect, however, in the homecoming sequence, as the false promises and seductive appeals of national identity receive their clearest embodiment and expression in the character of Kovic's mother. Emblem of both family ideals and national betrayal, the role of the mother focuses the contradictory interests of the text in an explicit way, embodying both positive and negative concepts of national identity.

As Kovic's mother comes to meet him for the first time since his paralyzing injury, the music swells in an emotional arc that is immediately countermanded by the distance and strain evident between mother and son. Unable to accept his condition, the mother, after a few inane and remarkably inadequate queries and responses, resolutely turns away from him. But while the mother is depicted as completely lacking in emotion and sympathy, the music accompanying this scene is unambiguously emotional and tender. The disparity between the musical accompaniment and the behavior of the characters expresses simultaneously the duality of recognition and misrecognition, of desire and estrangement, of intense feeling and socially defined roles that is at the heart of the first half of the film.

The conflicting signals that mark this scene as the obverse of a typical melodramatic homecoming reveal the larger historical message of the film. Kovic's "homecoming" will be deferred, the film implies, displaced to the end of the film, when the character and the society have undergone the transformative changes of the decade. Although the music underlines the significance the film assigns to notions of family, community, and "home," these themes are placed in the service of a historical argument concerning the changing face and nature of the nation. Oliver Stone's portrayal of Kovic's mother, which has been heavily criticized for its negativity, can be understood in this context. A kind of composite portrait of atavistic values, the mother represents the old America, the America of the fifties. Cut off from the "mother culture" after his wounding, Ron Kovic must find a new cultural, political, and sexual identity.

Thus, while the first half of the film emphasizes the melodramatic tropes of misrecognition and victimization, it also inverts some of melodrama's traditional sources of cultural authority, revising the role of the mother, community, and family. The mother, in particular, is painted as selfish and heartless, a "blood-seeker rather than a milk-giver," to use the words of Frederick Douglass.[26] This inversion might be seen as an aspect of the "double-voicing" that occurs when an older genre is fitted to a new context. In the Vietnam narrative, the nuclear family is a site of profound ambivalence, often depicted as both the cradle of hypocrisy and the matrix of positive forms of identity. In this case, as Pavel Medvedev says, "genre appraises reality, and reality clarifies genre."[27] The picture that *Born on the Fourth of July* presents of the malevolent influence of the family, a subject I address at greater length below, draws on the resources of melodrama, but it evokes the themes and motifs of the genre in a complicated way, in order partly to crystallize its rejection of the reality that it traditionally conveys. At the conclusion of the film, however, the nuclear family (and the image of the mother in particular) is restored as the emblem of a nation seen once again as a loving heartland. As we will see, this redemption of the maternal figure, and of the family, is expressly related to another of the resources and potentials of melodrama, namely, the rescue motif that organizes the second half of the film.

The Critique of Masculinity as "Punitive Agency"

As Geoffrey Nowell-Smith has pointed out, the link between doing and suffering, between action and passion—themes that were once securely joined—has been severed since the romantic period. In U.S. films, these roles have typically been separated into different genres, with male heroes "impervious to suffering" dominating genres such as the western and the action film, while female characters, "whose role it is to suffer," dominate melodrama. Suffering and impotence, the failure to act in the world, have been seen until very recently not as part of the human condition but rather as the consequences of a "failure to be male."[28] In contrast, *Born on the Fourth of July* foregrounds the co-presence of acting and suffering in a way that breaks the stereotype of the male hero. Although the resolution of the film links sexuality and social efficacy in a way that could probably be attained only by a male protagonist, the critique of the dominant cultural ideal of masculinity and the search for an alternative masculine identity are central elements of its social and political message. With its emphasis on sentiment and emotion, the film suggests not so much the patriarchal appropriation of a feminine mode of discourse, but rather a return to the Aristotelian definition of history as that which "Alcibiades did and suffered."[29]

While the search for alternative masculinities has been identified as a dominant motif of 1990s Hollywood films, *Born on the Fourth of July*, released in 1989, emblematizes the shift from the spectacular images of muscular masculinity that defined the films of the previous decade to a more internal, psychologically nuanced model of male identity. In a recent article, Susan Jeffords argues that the continuing decline of traditional sources of masculine authority, such as the workplace and the "national structure," has fueled a move away from the "highlighted masculinity"—masculinity as violent spectacle—that characterized the Reagan years to an exploration of male characters' "ethical dilemmas, emotional traumas, and psychological goals."[30] A parallel can be drawn to an earlier period, when the reformulation of national identity went hand in hand with the rejection of older models of male subjectivity. For example, Frederick Douglass, in his writings after the Civil War, explicitly rejected the "terse, masculine style" of his celebrated *Narrative of the Life of Frederick Douglass* in order to convey a different form of masculine and national identity; embracing a discourse of sentiment and emotion, he sought to transcend the association of freedom and liberty with masculinized, "punitive" agency. As one commentator on Douglass explains:

> Mastery, masculinity, and agency are often linked to death, so that, rhetorically, to gain a manhood guaranteed by violence, no matter how liberating, was to incur fracturing penalties that could tear "life" from "liberty." . . . Douglass used sentimentality [as a way] to conceive of [an] identity that does not require liberty to be divorced from life, or mother from child, male from female, subject from object. What Douglass tried to do was map a definition of "America" that did not require one to wield a whip.[31]

Something similar to this rewriting of masculine and American identity through the rhetoric of emotion occurs in *Born on the Fourth of July*. In dramatizing the transformation of a protagonist who defines himself, from the outset, along the archetypal lines of male power, the film brings together suffering and acting in a way that departs from American myths of the national hero, traditionally based on what Richard Slotkin calls "regeneration through violence."[32] Although *Born on the Fourth of July* begins with an image of omnipotent masculinity, it deliberately details the disintegration of this ideal, as the display of male prowess in its opening scenes is steadily replaced by representations of interiority that stress the main character's "sensitivities, trauma and burdens."[33] However, in its approach to what one critic calls the "dilemma of masculine subjectivity,"[34] the film oscillates between progressive and regressive ideas; it offers a searching critique of the relation between nationally sanctioned aggression and the construction of masculine identity, but ultimately resolves the "dilemma" of masculine identity by casting the character in the role of leader in the antiwar movement, dramatizing his political ascendancy in a scene that unmistakably echoes the combat "proving ground" of the generic war narrative.

Nevertheless, *Born on the Fourth of July* departs significantly from the oedipal scenario that for so many critics has become synonymous with male-focused narratives, especially those dealing with Vietnam and, more generally, combat and war.[35] Instead, the film offers a trajectory of masculine identity that does not depend on punitive definitions of agency or subjectivity. Although the rebelliousness and defiance of the main character appear to have an oedipal accent, the film, on the whole, is not centered on male rivalry or the substitution of one father figure for another. Unlike Oliver Stone's earlier film *Platoon*, *Born on the Fourth of July* revolves around definitions of masculine agency that are forged in relation to women, as it insistently plays out the metaphor of America as a woman. Although the rescue scenario that organizes the trajectory of the hero is fraught with limitations and patriarchal assumptions, it does mark a shift in gender roles and permits the film to question certain cultural definitions of masculinity. I would suggest that what Freud calls the rescue motif or rescue fantasy, which I discuss at greater length below, might constitute a fundamental underlying structure of the various narratives of masculinity, especially those involving Vietnam and its aftermath, that are currently being produced.

In first constructing the character of Ron Kovic as an avatar of masculinist mythology, the film seems to literalize the theme, sounded by Slotkin, that "myths reach out of the past to cripple, incapacitate, or strike down the living."[36] The thesis that American identity hinges on an ethos of violence is evoked from the opening scenes of the film, which feature Kovic as a child playing war games in the forest, noticing the disabled veterans of World War I being wheeled down the street during his hometown parade, and struggling, in a scene of slow-motion spectacle, against a superior male opponent in a wrestling match. The opening of the film illustrates the point made by Paul Willeman about the typical figuration of male characters in the cinema: "The viewer's experience is predicated on seeing the male 'exist' (that is walk, move, ride, fight) in and through cityscapes, landscapes, or more abstractly, history. And on the unquiet pleasure of seeing the male mutilated . . . and restored through violent brutality."[37]

The relation between male sexual identity and the warrior ethos is also made explicit at several key points. When the Marine recruitment team comes to Kovic's high school, for example, and the speaker begins boasting about the Marines accepting only "the best," Kovic is seen stealing a glance at his childhood sweetheart, Donna, who is walking by with another boy. Later, when he decides to enlist, he is shown discussing his decision with his friends while they pass around a copy of *Playboy*. The ideal of masculinity set up by the dominant culture is strenuously asserted throughout the first half of the film, but when Kovic persists in defining himself as the embodiment of the warrior ethos even after sustaining his paralyzing wound in Vietnam, the mes-

sage his broken body communicates recodes the masculinist ideology
he espouses into a message of self-destruction.

In *Born on the Fourth of July*, the wound suffered by the protagonist becomes the mark of a history that is not to be passed on, of a tradition to be resisted. The character's injury reveals to him a different
side of the national narrative; the national past is now perceived as an
unbroken chain of broken bodies extending from the disabled veterans
of the boyhood parade scene to the present. Although centered on the
character's internal struggle to recover his sexual identity—the dialogue is filled with references to castration, to not being a man, to
wanting to be whole again—the film brings into sharp focus the ideology of masculinity implicit in the military and national tradition he has
begun to reject. The character's wound has the effect of defamiliarizing
the various ideological props of masculine identity. The military, patriotism, sports, the family, religion, the profession—the various supports
and appurtenances of masculinity are overtly scrutinized and rejected.

The uncoupling of the character from the national narrative that
had defined him from birth is explicitly dramatized in the Fourth of
July celebration at which Kovic is honored for his service in Vietnam.
The film stages his breakdown in a highly symbolic fashion. Riding in
the hometown parade, a direct echo of the boyhood birthday celebration, Kovic finds himself wincing at the sound of firecrackers, de-
rided by young protesters, and demoralized by the long list of soldiers

from Massapequa killed in Vietnam. Called upon to address the towns-people, he is unable to muster the words that would link Vietnam and the sacrifices it entailed to a tradition of heroic endeavor. The sound of a baby crying in the crowd, together with the sound of a helicopter, triggers memories of the traumatic incident in Vietnam when his platoon fired on a village of women and children, and when he mistakenly shot and killed a man under his command. The linking of person and nation that has constructed the character as an emblem of patriotism from the beginning of the film here conveys an opposite meaning: to be born on the Fourth of July has become synonymous with murder and death.

Cutting directly from the failed Independence Day speech to a television newscast of protesters marching on the U.S. Capitol, the film pointedly juxtaposes the attenuated mythology of wartime heroism with the growing popular discontent with the war. The increasing occlusion of American society manifests itself in the living rooms, barrooms, hospitals, universities, and suburban streets of the film—former enclaves of social consensus that became, in the sixties, a new kind of border zone. The internal divisions of the period bring the liminal and contestatory character of national identity to the forefront, as if the borders marking the limits of the nation had been displaced to the center. In a sense, the character of Ron Kovic, at this point in the narrative, constructs himself as a kind of outsider in his own culture, a colonial subject living under the rule of a foreign power. Cut off from mainstream values, he becomes part of an America of "others." His alienation is expressed in a series of scenes in which he severs his ties with family, childhood, his hometown community, and the military tradition. At this prepolitical juncture, he defines himself principally by what he is not.

In the ensuing scenes, Kovic travels to Mexico, where he visits a seaside bordello that caters to the sexual needs of paralyzed veterans. Here, the film makes it clear that the crisis of masculinity the character experiences is really two crises: a shattering of male sexual identity caused by his paralysis and a more complicated, deeper loss of identity, the loss of affiliation with a larger social order, the loss of identification with the nation. In Mexico, Kovic attempts to recover a kind of physical authority based on the restoration of his sexual identity. Here, in a sequence that might be called the "virgin rebirth," Kovic has sex for the first time with a sympathetic prostitute and experiences a powerful sense of renewal and regeneration. But the brute, physical definition of masculinity that the character soon adopts—signified by the growth of facial hair, the eating of the worms from the bottoms of bottles of mescal, and the rather cynical use of prostitutes—quickly degenerates into exploitation and subjugation. The imagery of sex and renewal, emblematized in the full moon that illuminates his first lovemaking, gives way to the imagery of death. He begins experiencing flashbacks to the death of Corporal Wilson, the soldier he mistakenly killed in Vietnam in an incident of "friendly fire." In Kovic's memory, Wilson, who had been shot through the throat, is seen trying to speak, but the only sound that is heard is the crying of a baby, a memory-image that brings together not only the deaths of Wilson and the massacred women and children in Vietnam, but also, and more important, the identification of Kovic with the orphaned infant. The illusion of masculine power he constructs in Mexico is decoded by the unconscious into its opposite, a sense of infantile helplessness.

Significantly, the character returns in memory not to the incident of his own wounding, not to the point when his body was shattered and torn apart, but rather to the point when masculine power and aggression led to acts of villainy. Thus, the film situates Kovic's loss in the context of a larger failed narrative: the failure of Vietnam, the failure to accomplish the task, the failure to maintain mastery. Much of this section of the film revolves around the drama of the character's humiliation, his reversion to an infantile position. As Scott Benjamin King has

put it in a discussion of *Miami Vice*, "The male character take[s] on a role usually given to women: the ragged survivor of the narrative."[38]

Memory also plagues the other characters who have exiled themselves in Mexico. The illusion of fraternity, of an integral male world that the paralyzed veterans in Mexico try to sustain through poker games, feats of drinking, and sexual bravado, soon collapses into the naked expression of guilt and self-hatred. These themes come together in a powerful scene of self-excoriation, rendered, pointedly, in the form of a contest. After Kovic and his friend Charlie, another paralyzed veteran, are left alone on a rural Mexican road by a disgusted cab driver, they begin circling each other in their wheelchairs, spitting at each other and claiming, with vehemence, that they had each "put their soul on the line," that they had each fully experienced the horror of Vietnam, that they had each "killed babies too." They begin to wrestle in their wheelchairs, spitting, clawing, and cursing at one another, and wind up grappling in the ditch alongside the road. In this scene, the spectacle of masculine combat that so often serves as the climax of male film genres—the spectacle of the duel, the joust, the swordfight— is both invoked and inverted. The boyhood icons and ideals of the characters have come to this, the film suggests, to a desperate struggle against men who are their mirror image. Circling each other in a kind of helpless spiral, they express the trauma of their past experiences in the language of male aggression, a language of competition, one-upmanship, and ridicule.

After Vietnam, the film implies, the rituals and icons of male identity—the formation of masculine subjectivity in war games, varsity sports, and heroic physical prowess—acquire a different meaning. But what the film posits as an alternative masculine identity, one divorced from concepts of punitive agency, is highly problematic in its own right. As Steve Neale points out, images of masculinity in film are often caught between what he calls narcissistic authority, authority mainly based on physical power, control, and action (exemplified for Neale by the early Clint Eastwood films), and social authority, in which the male hero becomes identified with abstract values such as the law, the social order, and, by extension, the nation.[39] In *Born on the Fourth of July*, the male hero follows a similar trajectory from identity based on physical, phallic power and aggression to identity based on his ability, as one critic writes about a different film, to harness "phallic aggression to the ideas of freedom, brotherhood, and home."[40]

In the film's closing scenes, in which Kovic leads a protest at the Republican national convention in 1972, he assumes both attributes of masculine identity, serving as spokesman for the antiwar movement as well as strategizing and physically leading the storming of the security gate at the convention hall. Directly after, he is shown in the role of keynote speaker at the Democratic national convention in 1976. Here, we witness the acquisition of a new kind of phallic authority: the public and the private, the physical and the symbolic, the punitive and the

nonviolent senses of masculine identity come together at the end of the film in a way that asserts, above all, the paramount importance of leadership and individualism. Jeffords sees this type of resolution as an aspect of an emerging pattern in 1990s Hollywood films. Writing on the film *Terminator 2*, she says:

> Individual men . . . are made to seem not only effective but necessary, both to the protection of women and children and to the survival of humanity. . . . the power of individual decision-making and individual action is drawn as paramount. . . . Male viewers—particularly white male viewers—who may feel increasingly distanced from what they understand to be traditional male forms of power and privilege can be empowered through the assertions of the role male individualism must play in the future.[41]

Centered as it is on images of masculinity and codes of masculine behavior, it may seem somewhat surprising that *Born on the Fourth of July* confines its images of father figures to the biological father of Ron Kovic. In contrast to Kovic's mother, his father displays marked tenderness and heartfelt emotion at the fate of his son. As an alternative model of masculinity, however, Kovic's father lacks anything like social or phallic authority; he stands as a type of emasculated male, familiar from the films and television shows of the 1950s, a man whose emotionalism, combined with a lack of masculine authority, disqualifies him as an erotic object or as a figure of identification. The key relation of desire and identification remains that of the nation in *Born on the Fourth of July*, and its avatars are not the male characters of the text, but the female characters, who are vested with all the qualities of potency, destructiveness, ambivalence, and understanding that the text requires to re-create, through the agency of its hero, an ideal American homeland. As we will see, the restoration of the figure of the mother is essential to the establishment of this relation of desire. Repudiated by the text in previous scenes, the mother is elevated by the end of the film into a symbol of national ideals.

Imaging the Nation

Nations are commonly represented in the form of idealized feminine figures, but *Born on the Fourth of July* gives the metaphor of America as woman—more precisely, as mother—an unusual thematic and structural emphasis. Motivating the key events of the plot along the lines of the familial dynamic it implies, the film draws from this metaphor a scenario of nation as a wayward and misguided woman, whose salvation depends on the efforts of its hero.[42] With the title of the film signaling the importance of the maternal metaphor, we are led to notice both the consistency and range of the various images of motherhood the film presents. Three contrasting figurations of nation as woman are set forth by the film. Initially, Kovic's mother, like America itself, turns away from her son, unable to accept his physical and emotional condition. Later, in a scene set in the South, the film supplies a maternal figure who functions as an icon of forgiveness and understanding, an emblem of promised community, who sets aside her own pain to sympathize with the protagonist. Between these two images, that of the "blood-seeker" and the "milk-giver," the film introduces a third stereotype, pervasive in Vietnam representations—the whore— embodied in the Mexican prostitute who introduces the protagonist to carnal experience.[43] By inserting the figure of the whore into its maternal constellation—associating her with the mother in an explicit way— the film reveals the basic, underlying pattern of its narrative of nation: the dramatic and symbolic logic of the film rehearses, in close detail, what Freud calls the "rescue motif" or the rescue fantasy, in which a man imagines he can "rescue" the woman, sometimes seen as "degraded" or "unfaithful," by keeping her on a virtuous path.[44] In patterning its plot after the rescue fantasy, *Born on the Fourth of July* transforms its hero, the Vietnam veteran, into the savior of the nation, a resolution that recapitulates the evolution of the image of the Vietnam veteran in the films of the 1980s.[45]

In the process, however, the very myths of the nuclear family that had contributed to the war are redefined in the film as a solution to the disruptions of national community caused by the war. In this regard, the film is also symptomatic of a general tendency in Vietnam representations. As Rick Berg and John Carlos Rowe point out, the ideology of the nuclear family and the autonomous individual had much to do with the social problems of the Vietnam era. In the eighties, however, the nuclear family "began to look like a solution to the very political problems it had helped produce." Berg and Rowe make a critical point: "Rather than exploring just how our myths of the individual and the nuclear family had contributed to the war, the mass media focused instead on how our failure in Vietnam was reflected in the breakdown of the nuclear family and our loss of confidence in 'American individualism.'"[46] Vietnam was represented in the eighties mainly as a family trauma, embodied in the person of the psychologically disturbed veteran, who the family structure alone could cure. Even when the American family was not present in the narrative, anxiety about the family was nevertheless visible in a displaced form, shifted onto the Vietnamese peasant family. The massacre or murder of a peasant family, often with a Vietnamese child represented as the sole survivor, became a standard scene in these films. As Berg and Rowe aver, "The Vietnamese child came to represent, often in sustained close-up, what Americans had done to their own children."[47] Indeed, the Vietnamese peasant family in these films was constructed along the lines of a nostalgic image of a rural American past; generally showing them as country folk, with grandmother and grandfather prominently displayed, the depiction of the peasants "all too often looked more like life in Iowa than in Vietnam."[48]

Born on the Fourth of July adheres to this pattern in broad outline, including close-up shots of massacred peasants and a repeated traumatic memory scene of a newly orphaned Vietnamese child, but its analysis of the complicity of mainstream America in incubating the values and beliefs that allowed the war to occur sets it apart. The fundamental character of American life, with its stress on competition and individualism and its passion for authority in religion and politics, is held up to scrutiny. The family and the community are explicitly depicted in the first half of the film as the source and breeding ground of the national trauma of Vietnam, but at the film's conclusion the family and the community are portrayed as the medium of reintegration and, somewhat surprisingly, as the basis of political and historical change. Thus, the film seems to combine the elements of an acute critique with an endorsement of the essential morality and benevolence of the American people, who, when presented with the facts—or, in this case, the "confession" of the main character—are able to achieve a moral consensus.[49]

These themes are crystallized in the female figures in the text. The portrait of Kovic's mother, for example, stresses the ways in which she inculcates the very values of individualism, male dominance, and xenophobia in her son that will ultimately result in the tearing apart of the family, the community, and the nation. In the film's portrait of the mother as relentless ideologue—and she seems especially proud that her son will serve in Vietnam—it comes close to the imagery Frederick Douglass uses in describing the slaveholding nation of the pre-Civil War years as a "vampire" whose "most fertile fields drink daily of the warm blood of my outraged sisters."[50] Obsessed with fighting communism, convinced that the greatest threat to her son is his sexuality, and equating his athletic success with moral character, Kovic's mother is the conduit for the ideology of the dominant culture, showing the ways, as Berg and Rowe write, that the "middle class family reproduced domestically the values and attitudes of the public sphere."[51]

In its blending of the imagery of familial and political authority, *Born on the Fourth of July* illuminates the metaphors through which America conceives and represents itself. Whereas the destructive figure of the mother in the first part of the film serves as a powerful indictment of mainstream beliefs during the Vietnam era, the concluding scenes of the film feature a different sort of maternal figure, a character who condenses the attributes of an America perceived as an ideal homeland, a place where community is restored and where the veteran can once again assume a leading role. In many ways, the film ends up, as Berg and Rowe conclude about the fate of the Vietnam veteran in general, reaffirming the very institutions, familial and political, that led to the war in the first place. It reiterates the pattern of many Vietnam films in this regard, in which the isolation of the veteran is finally overcome in an image of communal redemption, where the conflict and division between individual memory and social coherence is resolved, and where the experience of the veteran serves as a kind of moral purification for the culture as a whole. As Michael Clark writes, "The critical implications . . . have been supplanted by a vision . . . that represents the veteran's presence in Vietnam as a memory of home; our collective relation to the past as a family reunion; and the restoration of the prodigal son as our national destiny."[52]

Prior to its final scenes of communal redemption, however, the film fashions another metaphor of nation in the scenes set in Mexico. Here, the demon/angel dualism described above is suspended for a time in favor of a highly unstable aggregation of the mother and the whore. In emphasizing the role of the Mexican prostitute, the film adheres to the standard iconography of the Vietnam narrative. The figure of the whore appears frequently in literature and films set in the Vietnam period, and is one of the genre's most heavily invested symbols. Alhtough usually depicted as a symbol of racial and sexual "otherness," the prostitute in Vietnam narratives actually functions as a textual nomad, a figure who migrates from a position of opposition to that of similarity, chiefly through her association with "American" values of commodity capitalism. In *Born on the Fourth of July*, the Mexican whore who first introduces Kovic to sexual experience is initially set out as the opposite of the film's maternal ideal: sensual, dark, and knowing. But the film creates a disturbing, and potentially incestuous, superimposition of mother and whore by having Kovic buy the prostitute a crucifix as a gift, an object strongly associated with Kovic's mother throughout the first half of the film. Directly after Kovic makes this purchase, however, as he prepares to present the prostitute with the gift, wrapped in paper decorated with hearts and stars, he sees her with another man, squeezing his crotch with seeming affection. As she later approaches Kovic's table, saying, "Today we get married, no?" his sense of betrayal is made apparent. From this point forward, the prostitutes at the brothel come to represent for him only dehumanized and anonymous sex, a point illustrated in a subjective tracking shot from Kovic's perspective as he wheels along a row of hookers, his eye directly level with their sexual organs.

In a sense, the whore in Mexico also represents America. The prostitute, like America, promises "happiness to everyone but [is] faithful to no one." The image of the prostitute, "vendor and commodity in one,"[53] recapitulates the image of America as soulless commercial profiteer, first conveyed in an earlier scene through the person of Kovic's childhood friend, who spends the Vietnam years building up his fast-food hamburger business (and cheating customers by selling burgers with concealed holes in their centers), for which he is accorded an honored place in the Independence Day parade. America, like woman, once had intrinsic value, the film seems to be saying, an intrinsic value that has been corrupted by money into a faithless and inauthentic version of itself.

It remains for Oliver Stone to redeem his image of America with another female stereotype, to resecure a traditional, virtuous concept of the homeland. And here we can plainly discern the contours of the Freudian rescue motif as the dominant underlying structure of the film, a fantasy that allows the character to "rescue" the nation, figured as a woman who has been turned from the path of true national character, while simultaneously being "rescued" himself, restored to the community as prodigal son and ultimately as paternal figure.

Freud describes a psychological pattern he calls the "rescue fantasy" in men who fall in love with prostitutes and whose erotic interest is dynamically linked to the need to experience jealousy. Typically, such men endeavor to "rescue" the love object by keeping her on the path of virtue. This type of behavior, according to Freud, stems from the "mother-complex"—an unresolved libidinal attachment to the mother. The unconscious correlation of mother and prostitute, which seems at first glance to be a relation "of the sharpest contrast," results from the child's first understanding of sexual intercourse, in which the mother appears to the child to be degraded by intercourse and also "unfaithful" to the child himself. Although the "love for a prostitute" that Freud regards as a neurotic symptom is one expression of this complex, childhood fantasies of rescuing the mother, or the father, are commonplace; Freud argues that when they revolve around the mother, they can be read as an expression of gratitude, a symbolic attempt to repay her for giving the child his life: "When a child hears that he owes his life to his parents, or that his mother gave him life, his feelings of tenderness unite with impulses which strive at power and independence, and they generate the wish to return this gift to the parents and to repay them with one of equal value."[54] The child thus forms the fantasy of rescuing the mother and saving her life.

Another way this wish is expressed is through the fantasy of giving her a child—"needless to say, one like himself." Here Freud makes an interesting distinction between rescue fantasies involving the father and those revolving around the mother. With the father, "it is as though the boy's defiance were to make him say: 'I want nothing from my father; I will give him back all I have cost him.'"[55] Rescuing him then becomes a way of squaring his account. This fantasy, Freud suggests, is commonly displaced onto other authority figures, such as a king, an emperor, or a president, and in this form often becomes a subject for creative writers (or creative filmmakers, as Stone's later *JFK* and Wolfgang Petersen's *In the Line of Fire* attest). When it concerns the father, the defiant meaning of the rescue fantasy is paramount, whereas with the mother, it is the tender meaning that is by far the most important, giving rise to the grateful wish of "giv[ing] her another life." Of course, giving his mother a child who most resembles himself allows the boy to identify himself completely with his father, in essence, to "find satisfaction in the wish to be his own father."[56]

In *Born on the Fourth of July*, however, it is the nation itself, symbolically represented as a mother, that is in need of rescuing. In the erotic relation that Stone and Kovic construct with the concept of America, the symbolic engendering of a new American homeland both allows the protagonist a paternal identity, completing the project of re-masculinization, and rescues and restores the character, in his role as wayward son, to the nuclear family and national community.

The scene at Corporal Wilson's family home in Venus, Georgia (the name of the town highlights the relation of desire that will be recovered here), captures these themes in a vivid way. After visiting Wilson's grave, Kovic arrives at the rural homestead and begins a conversation with Wilson's father. The father begins talking about the Marine color guard that came to bury his son, and about all the young men the town had lost. Leafing through a family album, he mentions that this town and his family in particular have a proud tradition, that Billy's great-grandfather was at the first Battle of Bull Run, his grandfather was in France during World War I, and that his family had fought "in every war this country's had." As if to underscore the point, Wilson's young son aims and shoots a toy rifle at Kovic. Kovic takes in the young son, the framed military medals in a glass case, the photos of dead ancestors, the deer's head on the wall, and begins to confess that it was he who had killed Wilson in the midst of an ambush, an incident of "friendly fire" very different from the story the family had been told

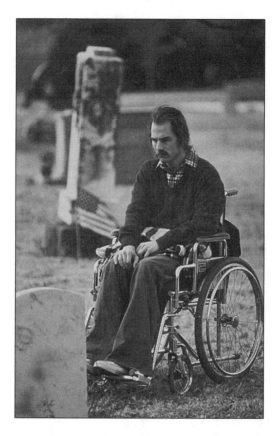

by the Marines. Wilson's mother forgives him, although Wilson's wife says she cannot.

The role of Wilson's mother is especially emphasized in this sequence, completing the maternal constellation, the three-way splitting of the maternal figure into demon, angel, and whore. As Kovic's re-memoration is heard, the mother is frequently seen in close-up, and it is her judgment that is appealed to at the end. Kovic himself appears in the role of surrogate son. The filtering of moral judgment through the maternal character restores the family structure to its dominant place. Whereas the myths of the nuclear family and the individual have been shown in the first half of the film to have contributed to the war, here, a family that had fought "in every war this country's had" serves as a synecdoche of communal redemption. The scene presents the rememoration of the protagonist as a source not just of individual expiation, but of a wider social purification, which will be completed in the scenes of violent protest and civil disobedience that immediately follow.

The leadership role that Kovic assumes immediately after this scene underscores the presence of the rescue motif, which is augmented by a series of historical parallels and references. As the Civil War song "When Johnny Comes Marching Home Again" is heard on the sound track, the scene at Wilson's home dissolves to a shot of the American flag, and then to a group of protesters in wheelchairs, arrayed in a way that recalls the "Yankee Doodle Dandy" fife and drum trio that often serves as an emblem of the Revolutionary War. The imagery of past struggles for national autonomy and identity is recontextualized to express a concept of nation and history as a site of recurrent social struggle. But more important, these historical references place the protagonist in the symbolic position of fathering the nation anew, according him a masculine form of agency that continues the legacy of the national heroes of the past. In the closing scenes of the film, Kovic claims the role of spokesman for the Vietnamese—"a proud people who have been struggling for independence over one thousand years"; for the paralyzed veterans—"Our wheelchairs, this is our steel—your Memorial Day on wheels. We are your Yankee Doodle Dandies come home"; and for the people of the United States—"white, black, brown, red, yellow," invoked by Ron Dellums at the Democratic convention, where Kovic addresses the crowd of delegates.

The ending of the film expresses both a sense of restored community and what Michael Clark calls "an ideal of historical continuity that turns Vietnam into just one more chapter in the epic narrative of the American dream."[57] As the character wheels himself to the podium, a series of flashbacks to his childhood appear. A past that had been synonymous with an order of destructive social uniformity is folded back into a utopian vision of a transformed social world. And the Vietnam veteran, no longer a divisive or menacing force, is here celebrated by the media and presented as a new kind of national hero.[58] The final lines of the film bring the familial telos of the work to completion, as Kovic says to an Asian American woman reporter: "We're home. I think maybe we're home." Rather than a point of cultural resistance, the memory of Vietnam has in the film's closing scenes become a new way of reinstating family and home as the dominant fantasy and metaphor of national community.

Conclusion

In its appeal to national identity based on the metaphor of America as a maternal social body, and its concomitant shift away from masculinist concepts of nation, *Born on the Fourth of July* exhibits a striking combination of blindness and insight. Replete with stereotypical images of femininity, the film nonetheless places substantial pressure on myths of masculinity that equate nationalism with competition and aggression. In trying to forge a new model of masculine identity that can serve as the basis of a changed concept of nation, the film sets out a trajectory for its male protagonist that may shed considerable light on the way masculinity is narrated and represented in films of the 1980s and 1990s. Film criticism has found in the oedipal scenario a nearly universal pattern for depictions of masculine subjectivity in the cinema, but I believe the rescue fantasy may be an equally important concept. In contrast to the oedipal scenario, with its consistent emphasis on rebelliousness, competition, and lack as necessary components of identity and desire, the rescue fantasy is shaped by a variety of emotions, including "tenderness, gratitude, lustfulness, defiance, and independence," a range that gives the "performance of the masculine," as it is commonly called today, a more balanced and complex character.[59] The shift from punitive concepts of masculine identity in the "remasculinizing" narratives of the eighties to narratives that emphasize emotion and "commitment" in the male-oriented films of the nineties might be analyzed not in terms of the fading of masculine authority, but rather as an attempt to gain access to the paternal position, by way of the rescue fantasy, without incurring the fracturing penalties of oedipal rivalry.

Nevertheless, the rescue fantasy remains a drama about power and powerlessness, and the organization of the fantasy, in its dominant version, around the figure of the woman who would be lost without the man's help clearly represents a fantasy of control. As such, this scenario hardly provides a progressive basis for a new narrative of national cohesion. Still, there is a certain degree of reversibility in the roles of male and female characters in *Born on the Fourth of July* that we should not ignore: Kovic is himself "rescued" several times in the film—from a morass of unfulfilled desire and self-pity by the Mexican prostitute; from corrosive guilt and self-loathing by Wilson's mother; and from physical danger, twice, by anonymous black men. In Freud's description of the fantasy, it appears that a certain reciprocity and role reversal is built in. The male child who wishes to rescue the mother is in effect reciprocating her, not just for the "gift of life" but also for being "rescued" by her from the dangers of birth: "The act of birth itself is the danger from which he was saved by his mother's efforts. Birth is both the first of all dangers to life and the prototype of all the later ones."[60]

Despite this quality of reciprocity, however, the rescue fantasy itself is fraught with ambivalence toward the figure of the mother, a point that *Born on the Fourth of July* makes explicit. As Miriam Hansen writes about Griffith's *Intolerance*, "The wish to be rescued revolves around the figure of the mother who, like Whitman's 'fierce old mother'. . . has displaced a failing patriarchal lineage with an even greater threat of chaos and loss of identity."[61] In similar fashion, the film's attempt to displace or revise the codes of masculine identity is ultimately limited and distorted by its use of maternal stereotypes as emblems of both division and community. Nevertheless, the prominence of the maternal figure in the film suggests that the theme of a "failing patriarchal lineage" in Vietnam narratives may express itself not only through symbolic conflict with the father, but also through a more complex negotiation with the imaginary power of the mother.

4 | Modernism and the Narrative of Nation in *JFK*

The debate over Oliver Stone's *JFK* has been framed to date largely within the discourse of historiography, with greatest attention being paid to issues concerning the limits of fact and fiction and the erosion of the presumed boundary between documentary and imaginative reconstruction.[1] Defenders of the film have usually argued from a deeply theoretical position, pointing out the permeable nature of the border between factual discourse and imaginative reconstruction, as well as the protean quality of even the most substantial documentary record of the past.[2] In this chapter, I wish to shift the angle of approach to the film in order to consider another set of questions, revolving chiefly around the tension between the film's formal innovations and its explicit aim to articulate a narrative of national cohesion. The film's fragmentary form can be revealingly seen as an expression of a national narrative in disorder and disarray, its collagelike narrative structure reflecting the disruption of the evolutionary or historical narrative that gives continuity to national identity. From this perspective, the film's notorious mixing of idioms conveys meanings that depart from issues of fact and fiction: rather, it expresses the fracturing of historical identity, the breaking apart of a once unified national text. The film thus recuperates its radically discontinuous style by linking it to the loss of what Benedict Anderson called social "unisonance," to the absence of a unified national narrative, which it nostalgically evokes as the foundation of community and the ground for all other narratives of human connection.[3]

The concept of nationalism has increasingly been tied to the development of particular narrative forms.[4] In writing of the nation as an "imagined community," for example, Anderson has linked the ideology of the modern nation to a specific sense of space and time expressed most clearly in the narrative forms of the realist novel. The temporal parallelism of the realist novel—the sense of temporal coincidence and simultaneity, of a multitude of unrelated actions occurring in a single community in what Walter Benjamin calls "homogeneous, empty time"—is directly related, in Anderson's view, to the image of the modern nation: "The idea of a sociological organism moving calendrically through homogeneous, empty time is a precise analogue of the idea of the nation, which is also conceived as a solid community moving steadily down (or up) in history."[5] Emerging as a strong form in tandem with the rise of nations, the realist novel, with its composite structure, its depiction of the one yet many of national life, and its temporal parallelism, "allowed people to imagine the special community that is the nation."[6] As Anderson says, the structure of the realist novel as well as the newspaper, both of which are crucial to the development of the imagined community, can be seen as forming a "complex gloss upon the word 'meanwhile.'"[7]

By contrast, Hayden White argues in a recent essay that modernist antinarrative techniques, characterized by fragmentation, the exploding of the conventions of the traditional tale, and the dissociation or splitting of narrative functions, may be the most appropriate techniques for representing the historical reality of the contemporary period, with its unprecedented catastrophes and its compound global contexts.[8] His hypothesis—that there is a deep connection between the cultural genres of modernist aesthetic practice and the social dramas of the twentieth century—provides a suggestive contrast with Anderson's ideas about the cultural models of the nation-building past. White argues that the stylistic techniques of modernism, far from being ahistorical or removed from history, as so many critics have contended, provide better instruments for representing the recent events of the past than do the storytelling conventions of traditional historians or, for that matter, the storytelling conventions of realism. Traditional forms of historical explanation, relying on concepts of human agency and causality, assume a kind of narrative omniscience over events that, by their scale and magnitude, elude a totalizing explanation. Modernist forms, in contrast, offer the possibility of representing, for the Western world, the traumatic events of the twentieth century, such as the two world wars, the Great Depression, and the use of genocide as a state policy, in a manner that does not pretend to contain or define them.

In these pages, I address the film *JFK* in terms of both of these models, hoping to show how *JFK* utilizes modernist, antinarrative techniques in order to express both the loss and the refiguration of a unified national identity. I argue that although the broken narratives and the profusion of stylistic forms in the film may seem at first appropriate to the catastrophic event of a presidential assassination and, indeed, convey a sense of a fractured social reality, they are ultimately recontained in a nostalgic image of social unisonance in the film's closing scenes.

The Temporality of Trauma

The disjointed temporality and dislocated spaces of *JFK* can be read as reflecting the distorted and irrational sense of national identity and the fragmented social reality that the film finds at the heart of the United States in the post-Kennedy era. Far from seeing the nation as a "solid community moving steadily down (or up) in history," the spatial, temporal, and narrative strategies of the film evoke division, rupture, and discontinuity between communities, between individuals and their actions, and between events and their causes. Analysis of the temporal register of the film in light of the idea of the nation as imagined community is especially revealing. The complex system of narrative temporality in *JFK*, to start with, is very far from the image of "homogeneous, empty time" filled up by the "steady, anonymous, simultaneous activity" conjured by the realist novel. Instead, the most striking characteristic of the film is its interweaving of past and present through an extraordinary combination of flashbacks, flashforwards, and achronic images—images that cannot be dated or assigned a temporal position. Moreover, time constitutes one of the principal thematic motifs in the film. Far from being seen as empty and homogeneous, time is thematized as heterogeneous and subject to human manipulation. Examples include the extensive newspaper report on Oswald that appeared in a New Zealand paper four hours before he was charged with Kennedy's murder; the *Life* magazine photo of Oswald with its contradictory times of day; the impossible chronology of Oswald's day on the date of the assassination; the delay in bringing Oswald down to the lobby of the jail, which allowed Jack Ruby to take his place among the crowd;

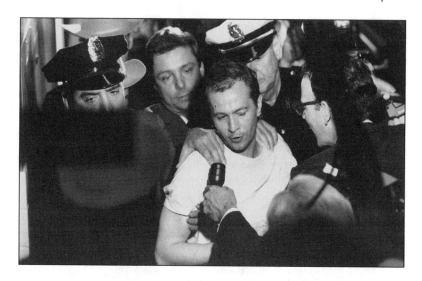

the phone lines into Washington that went out for hours immediately after the assassination; the live oak in Dealey Plaza that the Warren Commission claimed had unnaturally dropped its leaves in November, affording Oswald an unobstructed view; the shots themselves, with the Zapruder film serving as the "clock" of the assassination, giving the lie to the "magic bullet" theory, which would have us believe that a bullet could suspend itself in midflight for one and a half seconds. The overall picture of time that emerges is not one of uniform consistency, but of simultaneity corrupted by inexplicable delays, gaps, compressions, accelerations, and contradictions. Rather than fostering a sense of the security of parallel lives moving along the same trajectory, the film evokes time as a dimension that can be manipulated, a dimension that is open to doubt, ambiguity, and suspicion.

A comparison of two scenes in the film illustrates the close connection the text makes between structures of temporality and concepts of the national narrative and national identity. At the beginning of the film, time and date are specified exactly through voice-over, graphic titles, and overt period references. The historical portrait drawn by the film in its opening minutes depicts a society moving along parallel pathways in a homogeneous time, punctuated by clear-cut historical events. The re-creation of the assassination that occurs several minutes into the film furthers the impression of temporal simultaneity, as the time of day is foregrounded by numerous, almost obsessive, cutaways to the clock overlooking Dealey Plaza. Further, when Jim Garrison (the New Orleans district attorney whose investigation into the assassination serves as the basis of the film) is first introduced, directly after the gunshots, the time of the event is specified orally and underlined visually by rapid point-of-view cuts from Garrison's perspective to an antique clock. Throughout the opening sequences, then, the dominant temporal form is precisely that of simultaneity and parallelism. The film creates a snapshot of the nation at the moment of the assassination, forging a picture of a national community beset by tragedy, linked, as with the newspaper of the realist era, by the ubiquitous television broadcasts detailing the news of the assassination, the arrest of Oswald, and the swearing in of Johnson.

This sense of simultaneity and parallelism, the impression the film creates of a community drawn together by a singular, punctual event, begins to dissolve as the investigation into the assassination proceeds. As the past is opened up through a series of character narrations, the time scheme of the film becomes increasingly complex. For example, in the sequence that summarizes the various mysteries surrounding Oswald, several different layers of time are folded together. First, the scene begins in a reassuring, communal fashion, as Garrison and his staff gather in a favorite restaurant to discuss what they have found so far. A sense of solid, social reality dominates the opening of the sequence, as the maitre d' anticipates Garrison's request for a drink, which has already been poured for him, and as various well-wishers exchange greetings. Then, as the assistant D.A. on Garrison's staff discusses the oddities of Oswald's character, a summary of his life, consisting of black-and-white still photos, black-and-white film footage, and color "home movie" footage, appears as illustration. Periodically, however, another set of images is inserted: color footage of a mysterious hand fabricating the photo of Oswald with a rifle that will appear on the cover of *Life* magazine, an image that will seal Oswald's guilt in the eyes of the public.

In addition to mixing images that are manipulated or highly ambiguous with images that seem stable and thus imply facticity, the film constructs time here in a way that undermines any sense of its linearity, causality, or embeddedness in social reality. By interrupting the flashback chronicle of Oswald's life with scenes that detail the construction of a composite photograph of Oswald, the film stages the narrative of Oswald's life as a construct detached from the realm of everyday real-

ity and from the solid sense of social space insistently presented at the beginning of the scene. Social reality is abstracted and defamiliarized, as the submerged past that begins to surface here will lead Garrison to say, at the close of the sequence, "We're through the looking glass here. Black is white. White is black."

This is a pattern that will be followed throughout. The character narrations and subjective flashbacks defamiliarize social reality by narrating the past as a site of contradictory, mundane, and abstracted details, overarched by an almost biblical sense of prefiguration and fulfillment. As Garrison reads the testimony of the train yard manager, Lee Bowers, for example—a witness who spotted suspicious activities taking place on the grassy knoll—the film provides a series of images, attended by Bowers's verbal description, that are specified exactly according to time, place, and perspective. At the close of this narration, however, the film suddenly introduces a still photograph of the same man now dead, covered in blood and slumped over the wheel of a car. Only much later in the film will the suspicious circumstances of his death be revealed. Here, the film uses a technique of temporality similar, although not identical, to the Oswald fabrication scene described above: it telescopes time by inserting an achronic, undated, almost unreadable image, an image abstracted from any temporal or spatial connection with the rest of the sequence, into a series of images whose chronology is precisely specified. The mundane and the portentous, the particular and the prophetic (a textual motif underlined in the two Cassandra figures who inaugurate the film, Eisenhower and Rose Charmaine, the beaten woman who warns her doctors of the impending assassination), are placed in direct proximity in a way that transforms the past into something other than a horizontal cause-and-effect chain. The time scheme that dominates the film is one of anticipation within retroversion: flashbacks that also convey an instantaneous, but undatable, image of the future.[9]

Seen as a reflection of discontinuity and disorder in the national narrative, the temporal structure of *JFK* departs radically from the sense of continuity that traditionally defines the national past, and from the parallelism and simultaneity binding together, in Anderson's view, the community of the modern nation. The temporal collage the film sets up communicates instead the message that the national narrative has come unraveled, that the shots in Dealey Plaza have produced a caesura in the narrative of nation akin to the blackening of the screen that occurs in the film directly after the assassination. Many of the character narrations, moreover, come from socially marginal people whose testimony would not be seen as credible in a court of law: David Ferrie (a shadowy member of several extreme right-wing groups), Willie O'Keefe (a convicted homosexual prostitute), and the stripper from Jack Ruby's bar, for example, provide vivid and extensive character narrations, which, we are told, will carry very little weight in a legal proceeding. However, by looking to the marginalized and excluded as a source of authenticity and truth, the film implies that a split between the public sphere and the sphere of "the people" has further eroded the concept of nation as "imagined community."

If, as Timothy Brennan says, the nation is an imaginary construct that depends for its existence on an apparatus of cultural fictions, then the disjunctive, fragmentary form of *JFK* suggests the shattering of social identity.[10] It encodes stylistic characteristics such as fragmentation, rupture, repetition, and the atomistic scattering of details, as a sign of social morsellation, a mark of the falling apart of a once unitary nation. The message conveyed by the film's style thus intersects in complex ways with the positive argument, made by Hayden White, that modernist and postmodernist forms may provide the most effective methods for rendering the events of the recent past. Although the film vividly illustrates the thesis White elaborates—that historical reality far exceeds the capacity of any realist form to comprehend it—it nonethe-

less holds on to the very ideal of a coherent narrative of nation that its own formal structure seems to repudiate.

For White, the chief value of modernist techniques for representing the traumatic historical events of the twentieth century resides in the sense of doubt and uncertainty toward historical knowledge that a modernist approach to the past permits. Rather than assuming an illusory intellectual mastery over the event, a modernist style of historiography finds that the meaning of the past is contestable, because the questions we ask of the event cannot be answered with any semblance of mastery or totality. Historical reality itself has been transformed in the twentieth century, he argues, by the occurrence of events of such a compound nature and magnitude that any objective account or rational explanation based solely on "the facts" can only be illusory, implying mastery over events and contexts that escape explanation. The effort to come to grips with the "modernist" event can take place only in an atmosphere of historiographic doubt.

Although such a description clearly corresponds to *JFK*, with its mood of epistemological skepticism and lack of resolution, the film on the whole places a different kind of pressure on the question of modernism and historical representation. In terms of offering the cinematic equivalent of a sophisticated historiographic analysis, *JFK* is exemplary: it represents the event cubistically, from competing perspectives; it mixes film idioms, genres, and period styles (documentary, Soviet-style montage, Hollywood naturalism, and domestic melodrama, to name a few) in order to represent the variety of overlapping contexts in which the events occur; it foregrounds the artificial and provisional nature of any reconstruction of reality by refusing to predicate any single version of events. Nevertheless, in its overall concern for the relation between the past and an ongoing sense of national identity, the film seems to be split between its modernist form and its desire to reconstitute or recover a seamless national text. Although it uses the full panoply of modernist devices, it implies that a certain sense of history is part of the social imaginary, and that historical ambiguity raises deeply disturbing questions about identity.

Certainly *JFK* questions history both as a mode of knowledge and as a means of understanding the present. However, by focusing obsessively on a historical event, it also affirms a desperate need for history as the foundation of national identity. It has been said that "The interrogation of history is a stage in the search for identity."[11] Above all, *JFK* demonstrates the problematic nature of history in relation to identity, exposing the contradictory faces of a historical narrative that has ceased to function as an expression of the imagined community.

The images of history evoked by *JFK* can be described in terms of two competing paradigms. In the first instance, as a result of its obsession, *JFK* appears to represent a traditional view that a unified and fixed historical reality exists and could be recovered were it not obscured by willfully deceptive stories and by the inaccessibility of crucial facts. Seen in this way, the film sets itself the task of imposing a metanarrative to unify the disparate stories, rumors, and contexts of the Kennedy assassination into a coherent frame. At other points, however, and closely similar to White's concept of the "derealization" of the event in the twentieth century, the film seems to represent history as an "epistemic murk," an unstable discourse of fact and fiction, truth and illusion, that discloses only the scattered remains of contexts, motives, beliefs, and regimes of credibility.[12] From this perspective, the film's project might be described as an attempt to write a history that represents the incoherence, the contradictions, and the inconsistencies that characterize the historical text, exemplifying what we might call, with Homi Bhabha, the "dissolution of history as fragmentary composition; the decomposition of narrative voice."[13] The film's insistence on explaining the historical event, and thereby recovering a sense of the unisonance of the nation, is thus contradicted by its violent polyphony,

its filtering of the national history through the epistemic murk of rumor, fact, and illusion, conveyed through the complex temporality of the jump cut, the fast forward, the freeze frame, and the splitting of sound from image in which the past escapes any possibility of realignment in "homogeneous, empty time."

The Imagined Community as Lost Object

JFK oscillates between these competing paradigms, which are represented, more or less explicitly, in a series of character narrations. In place of social unisonance, the film provides a series of readings of the assassination drawn from a wide range of social types. From the almost freakishly marginal David Ferrie to the seemingly informed speculations of "X," these readings exhibit common characteristics as well as telling differences: they adhere to the same code of explanation, but make different appeals to belief. The confessional nature of Ferrie's account, the anguish and fear that permeates his monologue, conveys a strong sense of truth, underscored by the long-take camera work that seems to wish to offer itself as the equivalent of a visual polygraph test. By contrast, "X" offers the authority of an "inside view" and provides a sense of dispassionate analysis in which logic and history provide an explanatory framework. Juxtaposed in the film in a way that invites comparison, the narrations of Ferrie and of "X" exhibit a striking lack of unisonance at the level of the signifier.

Ferrie's narration, for example, stands out for the simplicity of its scenic construction. In a film characterized by virtuoso editing and stylistic "thickness," this scene is rendered in a straightforward presentation: there are no cutaways, inserts, or dramatized illustrations attending his description. Rather than establishing a unifying frame for the murder, however, a metanarrative that would resolve the incompatibilities of different texts and contexts, Ferrie offers a reading of the event that is polysemic: "It's a mystery, inside a riddle, wrapped in an enigma." He concludes by stressing the incomprehensibility of the event, its vastness and obscurity, a plot in which "everyone is always flipping sides" and in which the machinations of the Cubans, the CIA, and the Mob are described as "fun and games. It's all fun and games."

"X"'s narration, on the other hand, charts a different route into the social imaginary. Continuously framed with the monuments of Washington, D.C., behind him, "X" speaks of a plot that centers on the control, suppression, and manufacture of information. Cover stories, secret documents, conversations "in the wind" delineate a plot that has been rationally constructed from start to finish, and that could, it appears, be uncovered with sufficient access to "the facts." "X"'s narration, however, is replete with all the techniques that have garnered *JFK* such a notorious reputation for dissembling: it is filled with imaginary reenactments and recontextualized documentary images that dramatize a far-flung conspiracy emanating from the highest reaches of power. "X," unlike Ferrie, concludes by telling Garrison that Garrison can and must discover the truth, that his quest is "historical."

Drastically dissimilar appeals to belief are made in these readings: in one case, a straightforward scenic rendering of the character's version of events; in the other, a highly edited aggregation of existing footage, staged reenactments, and rumor made photographically concrete. In juxtaposing these two stories, both consisting of tenuous threads of information, the film exposes a cultural landscape in which different kinds of knowledge and different types of visual and verbal evidence abound. The different rhetorical strategies characterizing these two narrations of the plot to murder Kennedy, however, come together in a set of common dichotomies: both the testimony from "below" and the testimony from "above" shuttle between explanations based on personal acts of revenge versus collective political acts, between crime and subversion, between fanaticism and economic calculation, between inside agents and outside agitators.

Underlying the discourse about Kennedy's assassination, however, is the more elusive and oblique subject of the national narrative. In these two dialogues, different rhetorics of national identity or, more precisely, different metaphors and myths of the nation are placed in uneasy proximity. Ferrie uncovers one such myth in his "confession" that all he wanted was to become a Catholic priest, to live in a monastery, to pray to God. One of Anderson's central theses concerning national identity is that "the dawn of nationalism at the end of the eighteenth century coincide[d] with the dusk of religious modes of thought," and that nationalism essentially extended and modernized "religious imaginings," taking on religion's concern with death, continuity, community, and the desire for origins.[14] For Ferrie, the centrality and communalism of the church, especially that of the monastic life, stand as an example of collectivity only poorly replicated by the criminal and state-sponsored institutions that have replaced it. Ferrie seems to occupy in a complex way the position of the exile, nationalism's opposite. Referring to Oswald as a "wannabe, nobody really liked him," Ferrie brings to the surface of the text the desire for affiliation, for community, for the univocality of assent. The figure of the exile, seen here in the person of Ferrie as a type hovering around the periphery of the national community, is, however, displaced, in a paradoxical fashion, into the center of the film's portrait of national life, extending ultimately to the figure of Garrison, who will, like Ferrie, be metaphorically "defrocked" and banished, at least temporarily, from the national community—a point made apparent in the slanted media coverage of Garrison's case against Clay Shaw. Moreover, Garrison's identification with Ferrie is figured directly in the subsequent scene at Ferrie's apartment, in which Garrison looks into the mirror and imagines the circumstances of Ferrie's death. The dichotomy the film sets up between exile and the imagined community illuminates its narrative address:

the film posits its viewer as a charter member of the community of nation yet simultaneously alienated from it, both insider and outsider, winner and loser, part of the whole yet driven to reject the premises upon which the national community has lately been established.

A very different myth of the nation, and a very different sense of cultural identification, permeates the dialogue of "X." Here, the assassination of Kennedy is placed in a historical frame that encompasses not only the national narrative, but the principal symbols of national identity. Beginning at the Lincoln Memorial and ending at the eternal flame marking Kennedy's tomb, the sequence details a secret history, a national past that has uncannily woven itself into the communal text.[15] "X" narrates a history consisting of covert operations in Italy, Tibet, Vietnam, and Cuba that brutally extended and consolidated the reach of American power in the 1950s and early 1960s. The murder of Kennedy and the national narrative in general are described by "X" in terms of a universal imperial pattern: Caesar, the Crucifixion, the killing of kings are set out by "X" as the salient intertextual references for the U.S. narrative of nation.

Counterposed to this clandestine history of the national security state, however, is the implied narrative of national life represented by the monuments to Lincoln and Kennedy, who, the film suggests, are linked in a different chain of affiliation, connected to a different narrative of nation. This narrative of national life is referenced metonymi-

cally in the shots of two black children playing on the grassy embankment near Garrison and "X," and by the black father and son who are seen paying their respects at Kennedy's tomb at the end of the scene.[16] Blackness in *JFK* functions almost like a motif, the visible signs of an idealized national narrative characterized by racial and social progress, a narrative capable of binding the whole "national community" together. "X"'s version of the narrative of nation—"The organizing principle of any society is for war. The authority of a state over its people resides in its war powers"—appears to be contradicted by the mise-en-scène, which evokes a national mythology and a historical life of "the people" that appears to be distinct from the martial authority wielded by the state. The mise-en-scène of this sequence illustrates a point made by Bhabha: "The living principle of the people as that continual process by which the national life is redeemed . . . [t]he scraps, rags, and patches of daily life must be repeatedly turned into the signs of a national culture."[17]

Between these different representations of the national past and the national culture—one narrated, the other expressed through mise-en-scène—a major fissure exists. The imagined community portrayed in the film is clearly not fixed, visible, or unified horizontally, but is instead split into several separate and distinct nations: those "in the loop" and those who occupy the position of exile; those who are "faceless" and those who are marked by history. Split and divided, the idea of the nation becomes a kind of lost object in *JFK*, a unisonance once identified with patriotism and home—signified with exceptional nostalgic power in the lengthy montage scene that opens the film—now identified with loss and silence.

The imagined community as lost object—the modernist and postmodernist narrative techniques of the film express a sense of the splitting and division of a society, and of the loss of the idealized symbols of national identity. If the development of a coherent narrative mode is essential for achieving a sense of history and of cultural identity, as Anderson and others have argued, the film's antinarrative techniques would appear to signify identity's dissolution. If the realist novel is understood to serve a "nation-building function, equivalent to the institution of law," *JFK* would appear to display the divisions of culture, history, and symbolism that, the film implies, make our present sense of national identity so dissonant.[18]

On the other hand, the film's radically contestatory interpretation of the past can also be seen as a form of popular countermemory, bringing forms of popular cultural expression directly into the center of its narrative art. Bypassing the narrative forms of official culture, the film fuses vernacular idioms such as docudrama, television images, home movies, and grainy, tabloid-style still photographs to create a carnivalesque style of narrative texture replete with examples of "bad taste." The cultural and social landscape of late-twentieth-century America is embedded in the film's montage technique, through which, as Rowe and Schelling say, "different cultural worlds converge: a convergence of differences without uniformity."[19]

The nostalgic desire that permeates the film for a unified national culture, a culture of unisonance, a single national voice, is thus set against its modernist, montagist form, which draws on the multiple popular idioms of contemporary life. Cutting across the different social divisions and narratives of nation in the film, however, is the memory of violence, the memory of discontinuity emblematically figured in the death of Kennedy. In foregrounding the memory of violence, the film resists the reductiveness of a single, official history and defends the role and power of differentiated memories. Perhaps *JFK*'s greatest strength is its use of the disjunctive style of the contemporary media as an act of cultural resistance; it folds that message of cultural resistance into an appeal to national identity in a way that recognizes the media

as a terrain, analogous to the role of the novel and the newspaper in the past. But this strength might also be seen as the film's greatest weakness, for in the end this message returns us to the dominant narrative of nation and assimilates to national identity all other possibilities of community and solidarity.[20]

5 | Prosthetic Memory/National Memory: *Forrest Gump*

The extraordinary degree of contestation and debate circulating around recent interpretations of the American past has brought into view the powerful role that social memory plays in constructing concepts of nation. The public responses to recent museum exhibitions on the atomic bombing of Japan and the conquest of the American West, for example, have thrown into relief the radical differences between the interpretations of the national past offered by historians and the narratives of nation sustained in popular memory. Whereas social memory, as Michael Kammen notes, has long been uniquely divided from and joined to history in American culture—divided because the diverse and heterogeneous nature of American society gives us a multitude of memories, rather than a single unified memory; joined because the actual intermingling of cultures in American society gives us a history that hinges on memory[1]—social memory appears to have gained in value as a subject of public interest, while history, in the words of Thomas Elsaesser, "has become the very signifier of the inauthentic."[2] The rising importance and influence of social memory, moreover, has coincided with a widespread cultural desire to reexperience the past in material, sensuous ways, a drive that has been augmented by the mass media and the expanding reach of experiential museums and historical theme parks. With cinema and television increasingly drawn to historical subjects— examples include the advent of the History Channel on cable and the wide-screen success of films such as *Braveheart* and *Schindler's List*—

and with the growing popularity of experiential museums and historical reenactments—as exemplified by the Holocaust Museum and the
recent D-Day celebrations—the cultural desire to reexperience the past
in a sensuous form has become an important, perhaps decisive, factor
in the struggle to lay claim to what and how the nation remembers.

Walter Benjamin, in his famous artwork essay, describes the desire
of the masses to bring things close, to experience in a palpable, tangi-
ble way a relationship with objects and artifacts formerly venerated
from afar.[3] In my view, the contemporary desire to reexperience history
in a sensuous way speaks to an analogous desire to dispel the aura of
the past as object of professional historical contemplation and to restore it to the realm of affective experience in a form that is compara-
ble to sensual memory. The emergence of mass cultural technologies of
memory, moreover, provides vivid experiences of the past that can
shape and inform subjectivity. One writer has coined the striking term
"prosthetic memory" to describe the way mass cultural technologies of
memory enable individuals to experience, as if they were memories,
events through which they themselves did not live; the new modes of
experience, sensation, and history that are made available by American
mass culture, writes Alison Landsberg, "have profoundly altered the
individual's relationship to both their own memories and to the archive
of collective cultural memories." Defining prosthetic memory as "memories that circulate publicly, that are not organically based, but that are
nonetheless experienced with one's own body," she argues that prosthetic memories, especially those afforded by the cinema, "become part
of one's personal archive of experience."[4] Citing psychological investi-
gations from the 1930s on "emotional possession" as well as works by
Siegfried Kracauer and Steven Schaviro on the relation between film
and somatic response, Landsberg maintains that "the experience within
the movie theater and the memories that the cinema affords—despite
the fact that the spectator did not live through them—might be as significant in constructing, or deconstructing, the spectator's identity as
any experience that s/he actually lived through."[5] Although the production and dissemination of memories that are defined not by organic, individual experience but by simulation and reenactment are potentially dangerous, posing the threat of alienation and revisionism,
prosthetic memories also enable a sensuous engagement with past lives
and past experiences that, Landsberg argues, can serve as "the basis
for mediated collective identification."[6]

Memory and National Identity

The pervasive cultural desire to revivify the past through technologies and narratives of memory, moreover, may also be related to the contemporary crisis in national identity pervading late-twentieth-century American culture. At a moment of sweeping national redefinition such as the present, social memory and its technological variants may take on increased importance in the management of national identification, particularly when the national past harbors traumatic social experiences that have not been assimilated or integrated into the overall narrative of nation. As Elsaesser writes:

> What of the memory of events which live in the culture because of the images they have left, etched on our retinas, too painful to recall, too disturbing not to remember? "Do you remember the day Kennedy was shot?" really means "Do you remember the day you watched Kennedy being shot all day on television?" No longer is storytelling the culture's meaning-making response; an activity closer to therapeutic practice has taken over, with acts of re-telling, remembering, and repeating all pointing in the direction of obsession, fantasy, trauma.[7]

Elsaesser's example is a good illustration of the concept of prosthetic or mediated memory: even though the Zapruder film that he refers to was first shown to the public years after the assassination, it has become synonymous with the cultural memory of the event. Our individual and collective memories have been reconfigured by the Zapruder film; we imagine that it was part of our experience—we "remember" seeing the film when we "remember" our experience of the assassination. As this example indicates, film and media in the contemporary period have directly intervened in the cultural work of defining national memory, playing a key role in articulating and shaping the national viewpoint and debate around issues and events that have proven to be resistant to the larger projects of national construction and narrativization.

In this chapter, I consider the film *Forrest Gump* and its representation of the historical traumas of the 1960s as an example of the current preeminence of memory in the construction of concepts of nation and national belonging. In this film, the textuality of nation is expressed through memory; memory is thematized as the connective tissue that binds the lives of the characters to the narrative of nation, as

the webwork that supplies the forms and sites of identification that are essential to the emotions of national belonging. The film places in relief the power of memory and narratives of memory to create subjective connections to the national past, to call forth the sense of "I" and "we" that makes the national narrative compelling and meaningful. Moreover, it does so in a way that employs digital technology to "master" the past by "remastering" archival material, grafting the figure of the main character into historical film and television footage. But the positive value that the film accords memory as the modality of connection and belonging depends on a radical turning away from the historical register, understood as the broad spectrum of public events outside the archive of personal experience. The film conveys the message that history, seen in terms of public events and political conflicts, has somehow become disconnected from the authentic texture of national life, that it is detached from, rather than constitutive of, the narrative of nation.

In foregrounding memory as the connective tissue of nation, *Forrest Gump* appears to emphasize memory chiefly in order to construct an image of nation that can exist apart from, or float free of, the historical traumas of the 1960s and 1970s. The guileless hero, Gump, who comes across as a kind of national saint, narrates his own story in a way that emphasizes certain zones of social and cultural coherence within the deeply fractious social reality of the period, reordering the past in such a way that the political and social ruptures of the sixties can be reclaimed as sites of national identification. The film can thus be seen as an apparatus of memory that functions precisely like a prosthesis, supplementing or even replacing organic memory, which in the context of the sixties might be characterized as dysfunctional—cultural memories that in their organic form cannot be integrated into the larger projects of nation, that have been exceptionally difficult to assimilate. Social memory in *Forrest Gump* is in effect refunctioned in a way that allows it to be integrated into the traditional narrative of nation, producing an image of social consensus built around memory. What is sacrificed in this version of the national past, however, is the possibility of national identification built around history, understood, in the words of one writer, as the "chronicle of events driven by ideas that people have paid for with sacrifice."[8]

In using the concept of prosthetic memory, I depart from Landsberg's approach in one key respect: it is my argument that, rather than viewing prosthetic memory in the positive sense of creating an interface with "past lives, past experiences, past bodies" so as to ground individual subjectivities "in a world of experiences larger than one's own modal subjectivity,"[9] *Forrest Gump* revises existing cultural memory in such a way that it becomes prosthetically enhanced. Organic memory is refunctioned and redefined in *Forrest Gump* through mass media technology so as to produce an improved image of nation, at once potent, coherent, and "of the people"—a virtual nation in which the positive elements of national identification are segregated from the historical actions undertaken in its name. As Tom Conley aptly describes it, the project of national reclamation undertaken by *Forrest Gump* depends on the film's "wiping the slate clean of female presence" and on erasing the national canvas of social and, particularly, racial antagonism.[10] The film sets forth a narrative of memory whose transparent purpose seems to be that of "managing" the national traumas, the crises in national identity, that defined the sixties and seventies and that continue to trouble the nation's self-image.

Forrest Gump, the character, resembles nothing so much as the tattooed man of the Ray Bradbury story, a corporeal surface inscribed with the memory traces of a nation desperate to remake itself in the image of its remembered popular culture. Although history happens all around the character Gump—indeed, his life is shaped by it—his character seems impervious to the historical events that erupt in his immediate proximity. In the film *Forrest Gump*, nation is defined apart from history as a realm of mass cultural artifacts and experiences that are essentially detached from the traumas of the sixties and seventies. Although the period the film covers was one of the most divided and violent periods in the nation's history, the film gives its eponymous character the recuperative function of drawing from popular memory the filaments of a different past, a past defined by popular culture and mass media stereotypes, and implies that this past is in some ways more authentic, more in tune with the life of the people, than that of public history.

In evoking memory, however, as the register of national belonging, the film simultaneously erases many of the historical events that continue to trouble the national narrative. The national trauma of slavery and its aftermath, for example, is evoked in the beginning of the film as the source for Forrest Gump's name. As his first interlocutor, a black woman, sits on the bus stop bench that Gump occupies, he begins narrating the story of his life, which begins with his recollection of his ancestor, the "famous Civil War general Nathan Bedford Forrest," who "started up a club called the Ku Klux Klan." As Tom Hanks's face appears in a mock period photograph and becomes animate in what appears to be archival footage of Klan members on horseback that follows, Gump talks about how the club "liked to dress up in white sheets, and act like a bunch of ghosts or spooks or something; they even put sheets on their horses." Later, the history of racial conflict that the film invokes in its opening scenes intersects with Gump's own experiences, as his image is digitally inserted into newsreel footage of the integration of the University of Alabama. As the two black students walk into the classroom building over the protests of Governor George Wallace and under the protection of federal troops, the figure of Forrest Gump appears, digitally grafted into the newsreel footage, glancing into the camera. Then, in a staged sequence, Gump picks up a book one of the black students had dropped and hands it to her. He waves to the hostile crowd, and then follows her into the schoolhouse. In the logic of the film, Gump's insertion into archival images of a defining historical moment suggests a kind of reconciliation, a healing acceptance, one prompted, however, not by an understanding of the history of racial oppression but rather by a lack of understanding, by an absence of historical knowledge. Only Gump's ignorance, or feeble-mindedness, the film appears to suggest, protects him from the scarifications of history and the resulting distortions of character that plague most of the other figures who populate the film.

Directly following newsreel footage depicting the shooting of

George Wallace, the black woman who had been listening to Gump's narration leaves, and a white woman and her young son take her place as Gump's auditors. Gump continues his narration, which now centers on his experiences in the army and in Vietnam. Here, the film invokes many of the motifs and iconography that have by now become a kind of lingua franca of Vietnam representation, chiefly in order to invert their meaning: for example, the film emphasizes the interracial friendship of Gump and the black infantryman Bubba, reversing the standard imagery of racial hostility and segregation in Vietnam familiar from *Apocalypse Now*, *Platoon*, and other canonical texts; the film emphasizes the dedication and humanity of the commanding officer, Lieutenant Dan, ignoring the antagonism between officers and enlisted men that has become a staple of the genre; it stresses the heroism of Gump, who seems to have wandered out of a war film from the 1940s or 1950s in single-handedly rescuing most of his platoon. Signaling the trauma of Vietnam through rock music motifs such as Jimi Hendrix's recording of Bob Dylan's "All Along the Watchtower," the dramatized scenes in this part of the film are for the most part revisions of sequences from *Apocalypse Now*, *Platoon*, *Born on the Fourth of July*, and *Full Metal Jacket*. Parasitizing these films in a way that empties them of their original content, *Forrest Gump* in a sense "samples" the Vietnam genre and converts it to a different message.

The connection between war and national or counternational iden-

tification, a theme that is so thoroughly scrutinized in *Glory, Born on the Fourth of July*, and *Thunderheart*, is represented in *Forrest Gump* in a manner that is consistent with its rewriting of the terms of national belonging. The film explicitly alludes to *Born on the Fourth of July* in its portrait of Lieutenant Dan, who loses his legs in a firefight, and whose ancestors, like those of Corporal Wilson, the boy mistakenly shot by Ron Kovic in *Born on the Fourth of July*, "fought and died in every war this country's had." Giving a pointedly comic reading to the connection between war and nation, the film offers a montage of Lieutenant Dan's forebears, each in period military garb, each expiring on what looks like the same patch of ground. Lieutenant Dan, after being wounded in both legs and carried out of the jungle by Gump, protests that it is his destiny to die in battle, and that Gump is robbing him of his destiny. These scenes provide an almost mocking commentary on or counterpoint to *Born on the Fourth of July*, as Lieutenant Dan, like

Kovic, becomes a bitter, disaffected, wheelchair-bound ex-soldier. Un-like Kovic, however, Dan is not treated sympathetically in the film; his rage is at every point set against Gump's sweet incomprehension, which paradoxically seems the more valid and authentic response: the excruciating social and personal traumas of Vietnam are in effect noted but bracketed in the film, as if they are disconnected from the text of nation.

Nation and Religion

Gump's heroism on the field of battle is similarly disconnected from any metaphoric or symbolic concept of nation. Benedict Anderson points out that the imagined community of nation is in effect a replacement or extension of older religious ideologies, and that the concept of nation shares with religion the notion of a common cause greater than the self. National identification requires a willingness to fuse self-interest and the interests of the collective to a degree that only nation and religion have traditionally commanded. In that most powerful of national symbols, the Tomb of the Unknown Soldier, religious and national modes of belief coincide, Anderson writes, for here the willingness to die for one's country meets a mystical belief in the eternal nature of the nation, the belief in a collective destiny that supersedes the claims of individual existence.[11]

In *Forrest Gump*, however, this conception of nation is satirized and rejected; the history evoked by Lieutenant Dan and his putative destiny is seen as pathological, self-destructive, and ridiculous. Gump's

own heroism in rescuing his platoon is, in a sense, set against the script Lieutenant Dan wishes to follow: Gump claims he was simply following his sweetheart Jenny's advice—to keep on running. The fact that Gump misreads this advice in such a way as to become a war hero produces a complicated inflection of the Vietnam genre: the film rejects the war and the history it represents, but provides what may be the sole example of successful heroic action in the entire corpus of Vietnam films, thus projecting and extending a deeper narrative of nation, a narrative revolving around rescue. Later, serving as Gump's first mate on their shrimp boat, Lieutenant Dan will serve as the conduit for an explicit association of God and country, restoring the connection between nation and religion that was severed, in the view of the film, in the Vietnam War. Perched in the crow's nest during Hurricane Carmen, with the American flag whipping behind him, Dan rails against God, shouting that He "will never sink this boat." Then, after making a fortune due to the misfortune of the other shrimpers, Dan tells Gump that "I never did thank you for saving my life," and dives into a tranquil sea touched by a glowing, billowing cloud, revealing a large bumper sticker with the word "America" affixed to his wheelchair. Gump comments as Dan backstrokes contentedly in the water, "I think he made his peace with God."

Lieutenant Dan and Jenny, Gump's lifelong sweetheart, come to represent the twin avatars of a nation in peril, a nation in need of rescue. Posed opposite Lieutenant Dan on the cultural divide that defined the sixties, Jenny becomes a citizen of the counterculture; like Lieutenant Dan, Jenny is rescued by Gump both from physical danger and from a corrosive self-hatred. In the world of *Forrest Gump*, the counterculture is depicted as far more vicious and self-deluded than the military, as if the collectivist and utopian sensibility that suffused countercultural ideology were only a screen for male domination and posturing. In the film's portrait of the period, Jenny's body becomes a cultural battleground, a terrain on which is projected the competing cultural tendencies of the period. Her college dreams of becoming a folksinger, for example, are realized in the form of a nude performance of "Blowin' in the Wind" in a topless bar, for which she takes the stage name "Bobbie Dylan." Her involvement in the protest movement culminates in a march on Washington with her violent and abusive boyfriend, Wesley, the head of the Berkeley chapter of SDS (Students for a Democratic Society). She emerges from the sixties to become a strung-out disco queen in the seventies. Later, she becomes a loving mother, but she has contracted a virus that will soon kill her. The alternative national consciousness that emerged in the context of the counterculture is retained only in the music the film quotes from the period, rock songs that convey an emotional depth and cultural sensibility that the film insistently counterpoints to its dramatized scenes of male posturing and female exploitation, as if to undercut both the mythology of the counterculture and the music that provided its anthems.

The film's project of revising the cultural meaning of the 1960s is perhaps best expressed in the scene following the Washington protest rally. After receiving the Medal of Honor from President Johnson, in a ceremony at which Gump, digitally inserted into television footage, obliges LBJ's request to show him his wounded buttocks, Gump happens upon a mass protest at the Washington Monument and is reunited with Jenny. As he accompanies her to the headquarters of the protest movement, he meets a group of Black Panthers and Wesley, Jenny's New Left boyfriend. The Black Panthers harangue Gump, as does Wesley, who is incensed at Jenny's claiming friendship with a "babykiller." After a short argument, he strikes her hard in the face. The camera provides an ironic counterpoint by including in these shots a well-known symbol of the period, a poster with a raised fist and the slogan, "Power to the People" emblazoned on it. The camera fixes on Gump's reaction, then repeats the blow from Wesley in slow motion. As Gump then pounces on Wesley, the raised fist of the protest poster

is toppled and upended as Gump delivers several powerful punches. Here, the meaning of the poster is explicitly inverted: the symbolic fist becomes a real fist, directed at the most visible representative of the protest movement the film chooses to give us. The scene plays as a long-deferred rearguard reaction to the myths and rhetoric of the sixties, in which violence, in the film's reading of the period, appears to be the province of the counterculture, whose representatives wield, at various points, guns, billyclubs, and fists—in addition to peace signs and guitars—a perspective that substantially reorders the signs and meanings that have up to now defined the period.

History thus enters and marks the lives of Jenny and Lieutenant Dan, who together, as a kind of combined object, embody the loss of ideals, the loss of innocence, and the profound experience of spiritual and physical damage that the film associates with the national drama of the sixties. Untouched by history, Gump becomes an explicitly redemptive figure, a being who can address an antiwar rally on the way home from a ceremony awarding him the Medal of Honor, who defends Jenny and instills a sense of self-worth in Lieutenant Dan, who makes a fortune as a shrimp boat captain and showers wealth on the black community of shrimpers. The atomized qualities of an idealized national identity are consolidated in Gump, who is above all a figure of idealized continuity and connection, a figure who in the fantasy of-

fered by the film sutures the divided zones of American culture, intercalating black and white (the seafood company he founds is called "Bubba-Gump"), rural and urban (he becomes partners with Lieutenant Dan, a New Yorker), East and West, and who defines new zones of social coherence through his accidental influence on such disparate cultural icons as Elvis Presley and John Lennon.

As the national traumas continue to mount in the film's portrait of the period—the assassinations of the Kennedys, drugs, natural disasters, Watergate, AIDS—the character of Gump becomes a kind of allegorical figure of nation understood as an ideal, a holy innocent who wanders through 1960s and 1970s America erasing the sins of the historical past. At one point, Gump becomes a quasi-messiah whose followers believe that his running across America, several times over, articulates something of deep meaning and importance. As he strides past the barber shop in his hometown at the beginning of his marathon, we hear the ubiquitous television announce, "President Carter, suffering from heat exhaustion, collapsed in the arms . . ." After three years of continuous motion, running between sea and shining sea, Gump finds himself in Monument Valley, trailed by a group of disciples whom he has never addressed. Here, inscribed in a landscape that stands as a synecdoche for America, its fusion of narratives of progress and territorial conquest, and the projection of its mythology in films and advertising, Gump decides to stop running, as if to say the heroic narrative in which that landscape figures so large, the territorial imaginary that underpins the American narrative, had run its course. As

Gump's followers express frustration and confusion about what to do next, Gump decides to go home, a moment that seems to expunge the history of conquest and its theological alibi of providential guidance—themes that are encapsulated in the image of the prophet Gump in Monument Valley—in a personal epiphany of self-acceptance and self-healing. When he returns to his home, however, the film evokes, once again, the violence that seems to infect the public sphere, immediately announcing via another television broadcast the attempted assassination of President Reagan, thus bookending Gump's national pilgrimage with references to public events that seem entirely disconnected from the text of nation that has just unfolded beneath Gump's well-worn Nikes.

Redefining the Sixties

At this point in the film, Gump departs from the historical stage: his reunion with Jenny, their wedding ceremony, her death from an AIDS-like virus, and his quiet life with their son, Forrest, bring the film to its conclusion. What is interesting about this conclusion is what it implies about the cultural and social aftereffects of the sixties and seventies. In this counternarrative of the period, the women's movement, the civil rights movement, and the antiwar movement appear to be superseded in cultural significance by Gump-inspired innovations such as the "Shit Happens" bumper sticker, the smiley-face button, and the slogan "Have a nice day." The film ends with Gump describing to Jenny his life with young Forrest while standing over her frontier-style grave, as a flock of birds rise up from the fields in a kind of totemic recollection of her lifelong desire to become a bird so she could escape the miseries of her life. With the slate "wiped clean" of female presence, of racial others, and of social discord, the period can, in effect, be retrofitted to an emergent narrative of white male regeneration.

The reinscription and displacement of history in *Forrest Gump* memorializes certain aspects of the national past while creating critical amnesia in others. Its citations of public history are consistently juxtaposed to moments of personal crisis or renewal in ways that tend to displace the history evoked. For example, as a television newscast informs us that Squeaky Fromm has tried to shoot President Ford, a radio message comes through on Gump's boat to tell him that his mother is sick. Later, directly after Gump returns from his three-year marathon, we hear a news broadcast concerning the shooting of Presi-

dent Reagan, a moment that is eclipsed in importance by the letter from Jenny that Gump reads seconds later. Throughout the film, public history is depicted as the register of social unrest and political violence, a register that is essentially detached from the imagined community of nation.

In a sympathetic reading of the film, Vivian Sobchack writes that *Forrest Gump* invokes history as a form of paradox, marking a sharp distinction between the personal and the historical only in order to collapse this distinction and to conflate the personal and the historical, the trivial and the significant: "The complexity of diverse individual trajectories and their nodal coalescence in the massive 'historical events' we see foregrounded as the film's background are . . . undermined by the visible evidence that 'History' is the concatenated and reified effect of incoherent motives and chance convergences. . . . The temporally inflated notion of something we might once have called 'the historical event' is deflated and its specificity reduced to generalized matter." Sobchack argues that the film provides an especially acute rendering of divided cultural attitudes about history, a "symptom and gloss upon" a contemporary moment in which history, and historical consciousness, has been said to be "at an end," while at the same time becoming the object of unprecedented public interest and debate. "While one can certainly argue its marking the dissolution and 'end' of history . . . *Forrest Gump* can be argued also as marking . . . a new and pervasive self-consciousness about individual and social existence as an 'historical subject.'"[12]

Where Sobchack sees the film as engaging with the question of the role and importance of history in contemporary consciousness, I see *Forrest Gump* as framing a different set of cultural concerns revolving around national identity and the meaning and place of the sixties and seventies in national life. In a period in which the sixties have been startlingly reconfigured by some scholars as the source for the successful right-wing activism of the eighties and nineties,[13] *Forrest Gump* conveys in a singularly effective way the power of mediated memory to reorganize the historical past. In this case, it appears that the film evokes the cultural encyclopedia of the sixties and seventies chiefly in order to construct a virtual nation whose historical debts have all been forgiven and whose disabilities have been corrected. Although the film succeeds in defining broad zones of social coherence within a splintered national community through appeals to memory, it consigns to oblivion the most significant memory of all, the memory of historical agency that is the most enduring legacy of the sixties.

Conclusion

Throughout this volume, I have argued that the narratives of nation that sustain the cohesion of the imagined community are currently being reconfigured under the pressure of what might be called the "recovered memory" of the American nation-state, a recovery that has occasioned widespread public debate about the traumatic events of the national past. The historical traumas of the past—slavery, the genocide of Native Americans, the assassination of President Kennedy, the Vietnam War—have now emerged as important catalysts of cultural redefinition, evidenced in the extraordinary degree of contestation and debate circulating around current historical films that deal with these events, and in controversies over recent museum exhibitions and commemorative reenactments. Although the current debate over the way the national past is represented cuts across a range of political, ideological, generational, and racial issues, one theme stands out as a consistent feature of recent attempts to narrate the nation: the importance of social or popular memory within American culture, a form of memory that speaks to an affective and emotional understanding of the past that is frequently at odds with public, official history. The ongoing recovery of historical experiences that have been excluded from dominant accounts is one example of the assertion of social memory against the forms of traditional history; another example, from a different angle, is the insistent defense by the dominant classes of a historical narrative that professional historians have largely rejected, seen most

120

clearly in the resistance to the planned Smithsonian exhibition com-memorating, but also questioning, the atomic bombing of Japan. In the conflict over the interrogation of the national past, a deep-rooted struggle over concepts of national identity can be discerned, a struggle that bears on fundamental issues of national definition and that ulti-mately raises questions about the very possibility of a plenary narrative of nation.

This question is brought to the fore in *Forrest Gump*, which in many ways can be seen as the bald antithesis of the themes and ideas that have motivated the major part of this text. *Forrest Gump* attempts to redefine the cultural fictions of nation in the late twentieth century in ways that in the main explicitly contradict the historical arguments of the films that I analyze in earlier chapters; rather than recovering the historical experiences of people marginalized in dominant accounts, *Forrest Gump* erases or diminishes these strands of the national text; rather than defining nation in terms of the torsion among differing concepts of identity, the film associates the imagined community of na-tion with the saintly singularity of identity embodied in Gump; rather than rewriting the dominant fiction to reflect the polycultural inter-dependence of American life, the film aggressively attempts to restore the mythology of agrarianism, self-reliance, and providential guidance that forms the core of the traditional narrative of nation.

Nevertheless, when considered in terms of a dialogic encounter with *Born on the Fourth of July*, *JFK*, *Glory*, and *Thunderheart*, some of which it evokes explicitly, *Forrest Gump* brings into view the high cultural stakes of the current cinematic struggle to redefine the na-tional text. More than ever, contemporary films function as an ideolog-ical force seeking to refashion national identity. The conflicted views of the American past that these films throw into relief are part of an on-going rewriting of the foundational texts of nation. In *Glory*, for ex-ample, present-day race relations are reconsidered through its rewrit-ing of the Civil War, wherein the white perspective of Yankee New England that has dominated treatments of the period is reshaped by the encounter with a more supple black conception of history, lan-guage, and fraternity. In *Thunderheart*, the Native American past is re-vivified through the memory of struggles at Wounded Knee. By con-trast, *JFK* disinters and explodes the different interpretations of the Kennedy assassination in order to question our understanding of the national past. *Born on the Fourth of July* rehearses the war film genre and complicates the genre's traditional message of patriotic violence as the basis of national identification. *Forrest Gump*, for its part, responds to the wrenching scrutiny of national traumas that these films unfold with an even greater quotient of violence, erasing blacks, women, and the seismic changes associated with the 1960s and 1970s in a traumatized closing down of historical inquiry. Refashioning what it takes to be the authentic texture of nation around popular memory evacuated of political meaning, the film appeals to memory in order to create amnesia in other areas.

The point I would like to emphasize here, however, is the way *Forrest Gump* confirms the changes in the national narrative and in the identity of nation that it aggressively seeks to cloak in oblivion. Its appeal to a form of ethnic nostalgia, to what Michael Ignatieff calls blood and belonging, betrays a melancholy sense of the game having been lost, as if the film, like the character, had somehow missed the point. The extraordinary popularity and institutional success of *Forrest Gump* underline the anxiety that marks the current struggle over ethnicity and race, over gender, over region, and over interpretations of the national past, for which the film offers a kind of narcotic. On the positive side, however, it highlights, like a Freudian slip of the tongue, the degree to which the imagined community of nation resonates in the private as well as the public sphere. And it locates, with greater insight than one might expect, the central role that the cinema plays in the imaging of nation.

Notes

Introduction

1. Jacques Rancière, "Interview: The Image of Brotherhood," trans. Kari Hanet, *Edinburgh '77 Magazine*, no. 2 (1977): 26–31. Kaja Silverman expands on Rancière's concept of the dominant fiction in *Male Subjectivity at the Margins* (New York: Routledge, 1992): see especially 15–121.

2. Rancière, "The Image of Brotherhood."

3. Timothy Brennan, "The National Longing for Form," in *Nation and Narration*, ed. Homi K. Bhabha (London: Routledge, 1990): 49. See also Benedict Anderson, *Imagined Communities: Reflections on the Origin and Spread of Nationalism* (London: Verso, 1991).

4. Rancière, "The Image of Brotherhood."

5. See Roy Harvey Pearce, *Savagism and Civilization: A Study of the Indian and the American Mind* (Berkeley: University of California Press, 1988): 49.

6. The concept of nation as an "imagined community" has been set forth by Anderson in *Imagined Communities*. The phrase "deep, horizontal comradeship" comes from Ellis Cashmore, *Dictionary of Race and Race Relations* (London: Routledge, 1984).

7. Virginia Wright Wexman, *Creating the Couple: Love, Marriage, and Hollywood Performance* (Princeton, N.J.: Princeton University Press, 1993): 72.

8. Cornel West characterizes competing forms of identity in terms of "identity from above" and "identity from below" in "A Matter of Life and Death," *October* 61 (Summer 1992): 20–23.

9. Michael Kammen, *The Mystic Chords of Memory: The Transformation of Tradition in American Culture* (New York: Knopf, 1991): 299.

10. Ibid.

11. Ibid., 688.

12. Examples include the advent of the History Channel on cable and the success of Ken Burns's documentaries on public television.

13. George Lipsitz, *Time Passages: Collective Memory and American Popular Culture* (Minneapolis: University of Minnesota Press, 1990): 4.

14. Ibid., 36.

15. Caryn James, "These Are Works of Art, Not Children's Schoolbooks," *New York Times*, May 21, 1995: 18.

16. Ibid.

17. Victor Turner, "Social Dramas and Stories about Them," *Critical Inquiry* 7 (1980): 168.

18. Nathan Huggins, "The Deforming Mirror of Truth: Slavery and the Master Narrative of American History," *Radical History Review* (Winter 1991): 37.

19. The phrase "fissures and faultlines" comes from Wimal Dissanayake, "Nationhood, History, and Cinema: Reflections on the Asian Scene," in *Colonialism and Nationalism in Asian Cinema*, ed. Wimal Dissanayake (Bloomington: Indiana University Press, 1994).

20. Although Hollywood defines itself purely as an entertainment industry, in contrast to the film industries of countries such as France, Canada, and Australia, which serve a semiofficial role as the "cultural flagships" of their nations, the Hollywood cinema, taken as a whole, can be seen to express both the mythic and the prosaic dimensions of nation. Although no single film or genre could be said to capture all the tributaries of national life, the Hollywood genre system as a whole functions as a kind of vast *speculum mundi* that defines what passes as social reality in the United States. As Fredric Jameson writes: "The reality socially constructed by Hollywood 'realism' is a map whose coordinates are parcelled out among the specific genres, to whose distinct registers are assigned its various dimensions or specialized segments. The 'world' is then not what is represented in the romantic comedy or in film noir: but it is what is somehow governed by all of them together—the musical, the gangster cycles, 'screwball comedy,' melodrama. . . . The unreal is then what falls outside of the system as a whole and finds no place in it." Fredric Jameson, *Signatures of the Visible* (New York: Routledge, 1990): 175–76. Although Jameson does not refer specifically to the concept of national identity and restricts his description to the classic period of the Hollywood studio system, the model he sets forth can, I believe, be adapted to the question of the American cinema's role in constructing concepts of nation. If, as Brennan describes it in "The National Longing for Form," the nation is an "imaginary construct" that depends for its existence on an "apparatus of cultural fictions," that apparatus in the present-day United States is centered in the Hollywood cinema.

21. See Annette Hamilton, "Fear and Desire: Aborigines, Asians, and the National Imaginary," *Australian Cultural History* 9 (1990): 18.

22. For discussion of the concept of "genre memory," see Gary Saul Morson and Caryl Emerson, *Mikhail Bakhtin: The Creation of a Prosaics* (Stanford, Calif.: Stanford University Press, 1990).

23. In *Imagined Communities*, Anderson argues that the realist novel, which rose to prominence in tandem with the rise of the nation-state, is the most exemplary manifestation of national self-consciousness, for it resembles in its form and structure the multiplicity and simultaneity of national life. With its mixture of idioms, its composite structure, and its use of temporal parallelism as a way of linking a multitude of unrelated actions, the realist novel provided people with an image of nation as a "solid community" moving simultaneously up or down through history, of parallel lives moving along parallel pathways, a structure that "allowed people to imagine the special community that is the nation" (25).

24. Anthony D. Smith, "War and Ethnicity: The Role of Warfare in the Formation,

Self-Images, and Cohesion of Ethnic Communities," *Ethnic and Racial Studies* 4, no. 4 (1981): 391.

25. Morson and Emerson, *Mikhail Bakhtin*, 290, 292, 278, 293, 297.

26. Smith, "War and Ethnicity," 391.

27. Michael Ignatieff, *Blood and Belonging: Journeys into the New Nationalism* (New York: Farrar, Straus & Giroux, 1993): 6.

28. See ibid. and Anthony D. Smith, *National Identity* (Reno: University of Nevada Press, 1991).

29. Ignatieff, *Blood and Belonging*, 5, 9.

30. Smith, *National Identity*, 15.

31. The concept of polycentric or pluralistic nationalism is developed in Yael Tamir, *Liberal Nationalism* (Princeton, N.J.: Princeton University Press, 1993). She derives the phrase "polycentric nationalism" from Anthony D. Smith, *Theories of Nationalism* (London: Duckworth, 1983).

32. Ignatieff, *Blood and Belonging*, 248.

33. John D. Kelly, "Diaspora and World War, Blood and Nation in Fiji and Hawaii," *Public Culture* 7, no. 3 (1995): 489.

34. Ibid., 495.

35. Homi K. Bhabha, "DissemiNation: Time, Narrative, and the Margins of the Modern Nation," in *Nation and Narration*, ed. Homi K. Bhabha (London: Routledge, 1990): 318.

36. Michael Ignatieff, "The State of Belonging," *Time*, February 27, 1995: 56.

37. Dissanayake, "Nationhood, History, and Cinema," xvi.

38. Iain Chambers, *Border Dialogues: Journeys in Postmodernism* (London: Routledge, 1990): 47.

39. Graeme Turner, "The End of the National Project? Australian Cinema in the 1990's," in *Colonialism and Nationalism in the Asian Cinema*, ed. Wimal Dissanayake (Bloomington: Indiana University Press, 1994): 214.

40. Ignatieff, *Blood and Belonging*, 249.

41. This passage combines phrases from Peter H. Wood, "Response to Nathan Huggins's 'The Deforming Mirror of Truth,'" *Radical History Review* (Winter 1991): 53; and Huggins, "The Deforming Mirror," 45, 39.

42. Hamilton, "Fear and Desire."

43. Susan Jeffords, *The Remasculinization of America: Gender and the Vietnam War* (Bloomington: Indiana University Press, 1989).

44. Hayden White, "The Fact of Modernism: The Fading of the Historical Event," in *The Persistence of History: Cinema, Television, and the Modern Event*, ed. Vivian Sobchack (New York: Routledge, 1995).

1. Race and Nation in *Glory*

1. Michael Ignatieff, *Blood and Belonging: Journeys into the New Nationalism* (New York: Farrar, Straus & Giroux, 1993).

2. Cornel West, "A Matter of Life and Death," *October* 61 (Summer 1992): 20–23.

3. Paul Gilroy, *There Ain't No Black in the Union Jack* (London: Hutchinson, 1987): 52.

4. Peter Dimock, "Towards a Social Narrative of Loss," *Radical History Review* (Winter 1991): 54–56.

5. Richard Dyer, "White," in *The Matter of Images: Essays on Representations* (London: Routledge, 1993): 145.

6. Ibid., 141.

7. Ibid., 144.

8. Edward Zwick, the director of *Glory*, is probably best known as the cocreator of the TV series *thirtysomething*. In an interview in *Film Comment*, he describes the "anachronistic" scene in which Trip and Shaw converse about their parallel purposes as containing "a certain degree of liberal fantasy." See Armond White, "Fighting Black," *Film Comment* (January–February 1990): 26.

9. Frederick Douglass, *The Life and Writing of Frederick Douglass*, vol. 3 (New York: International, 1953): "The iron gate of our prison stands half open . . . one gallant rush . . . will fling it wide" (123).

10. Gary Scharnhorst, "From Soldier to Saint: Robert Gould Shaw and the Rhetoric of Racial Justice," *Civil War History* 34, no. 4 (1988): 308–22.

11. Ibid., 317–18.

12. See Peter Burchard, *One Gallant Rush* (New York: St. Martin's, 1965): on Douglass's sons, see 84, 139; on Charlotte Forten, see 116–17, 145–46. In the film, the black woman standing near Shaw in the Port Royal scene is, according to the screenwriter, Kevin Jarre, meant to represent Charlotte Forten.

13. Nathan Huggins, "The Deforming Mirror of Truth: Slavery and the Master Narrative of American History," *Radical History Review* (Winter 1991): 37.

14. Frederick Douglass, *My Bondage and My Freedom*, ed. William L. Andrews (Urbana: University of Illinois Press, 1987): 218–19.

15. Huggins, "The Deforming Mirror," 25.

16. Ibid., 38.

17. Frantz Fanon, *The Wretched of the Earth* (New York: Grove Weidenfeld, 1968): 51–53.

18. Homi K. Bhabha, "A Question of Survival: Nations and Psychic States," in *Psychoanalysis and Cultural Theory: Thresholds*, ed. James Donald (London: Macmillan, 1991): 98–99.

19. Ibid., 99.

20. Douglass, *My Bondage*, 218–19.

21. Huggins, "The Deforming Mirror," 31.

22. Frederick Douglass, *Narrative of the Life of Frederick Douglass, American Slave, as Written by Himself*, ed. Houston A. Baker Jr. (New York: Penguin American Library, 1982): 72; quoted in Stephanie A. Smith, "Heart Attacks: Frederick Douglass's Strategic Sentimentality," *Criticism* 34, no. 2 (1992): 197.

23. Mikhail Bakhtin, quoted in Gary Saul Morson and Caryl Emerson, *Mikhail Bakhtin: Creation of a Prosaics* (Stanford, Calif.: Stanford University Press, 1990): 411.

24. See White, "Fighting Black."

25. See Lawrence W. Levine, "Slave Songs and Slave Consciousness: An Exploration of Forgotten Sources," in *Anonymous Americans: Explorations in Nineteenth-Century Social History*, ed. Tamara K. Hareven (Englewood Cliffs, N.J.: Prentice Hall, 1971): 99–130.

26. Gilroy, *There Ain't No Black*, 159.

27. Levine, "Slave Songs," 120.

28. Stuart Hall, "Minimal Selves," in *Identity: The Real Me* (London: ICA, 1987): 45.

29. Gilroy, *There Ain't No Black*, 236.

30. Huggins, "The Deforming Mirror," 38.

31. Gilroy, *There Ain't No Black*, 26.

32. Raymond Williams, *Towards 2000* (Harmondsworth: Penguin, 1983); quoted in ibid., 50.

33. Variations of this phrase appear in Huggins, "The Deforming Mirror," and the separate "Responses" of Peter H. Wood, Peter Dimock, and Barbara Clark Smith, *Radical History Review* (Winter 1991): 25–59.

2. Native America, *Thunderheart,* and the National Imaginary

1. Edward H. Spicer, "The Nations of a State," *Boundary 2* 19, no. 3 (1992): 26–48.

2. The quoted phrases are from ibid.

3. Annette Hamilton, "Fear and Desire: Aborigines, Asians, and the National Imaginary," *Australian Cultural History* 9 (1990): 14–35.

4. Nicholas Colchester, "Goodbye, Nation-State. Hello . . . What?" *New York Times*, July 17, 1994: 17.

5. Hamilton, "Fear and Desire," 16.

6. Ibid., 23.

7. Michael P. Rogin, *Ronald Reagan, the Movie, and Other Episodes in Political Demonology* (Berkeley: University of California Press, 1987): 141, 138, 146. See generally Rogin's chapter titled "Liberal Society and the Indian Question," 134–68.

8. Lauren Berlant, *The Anatomy of National Fantasy: Hawthorne, Utopia, and Everyday Life* (Chicago: University of Chicago Press, 1991): 217.

9. Arnold Krupat, "Postcoloniality and Native American Literature," *Yale Journal of Criticism* 7, no. 1 (1994): 175.

10. Ward Churchill, *Fantasies of the Master Race: Literature, Cinema and the Colonization of American Indians* (Monroe, Maine: Common Courage, 1992): 242–43.

11. Gary Saul Morson and Caryl Emerson, *Mikhail Bakhtin: The Creation of a Prosaics* (Stanford, Calif.: Stanford University Press, 1990): 290–92.

12. Hamilton, "Fear and Desire," 18.

13. Benedict Anderson, *Imagined Communities: Reflections on the Origin and Spread of Nationalism* (London: Verso, 1991): 26, 25; see generally 9–36.

14. Fernand Braudel, "History and the Social Sciences: The Long Duree," in *On History*, trans. Sarah Matthews (Chicago: University of Chicago Press, 1980): 26–27.

15. Elaine A. Jahner, "Transitional Narratives and Cultural Continuity," *Boundary 2* 19, no. 3 (1992): 169; see also Anderson, *Imagined Communities*, 9–36.

16. The concept of heterochrony is discussed at length in Morson and Emerson, *Mikhail Bakhtin*.

17. Krupat, "Postcoloniality," 175.

18. Roy Harvey Pearce, *Savagism and Civilization: A Study of the Indian and the American Mind* (Berkeley: University of California Press, 1988): 49.

19. Edward Said, "Identity, Negation, and Violence," *New Left Review* 171 (1988): 58; quoted in Krupat, "Postcoloniality," 175.

20 Krupat, "Postcoloniality," 175.

21. Anthony D. Smith, "War and Ethnicity: The Role of Warfare in the Formation, Self-Images, and Cohesion of Ethnic Communities," *Ethnic and Racial Studies* 4, no. 4 (1981): 391.

22. The plot of the film is closely based on a series of incidents that occurred on and near the Pine Ridge Reservation in the mid-1970s, the site of a growing activist movement led by traditional Lakotas trying to regain control of tribal lands. The corrupt tribal government of Richard Wilson, installed by the federal authorities, tried to suppress this move-

ment through a campaign of terror waged by Wilson's private army, widely known by the acronym GOON (Guardians of the Oglala Nation). In order to deal with GOON violence, and to prevent the illegal transfer of uranium-rich reservation land to the federal government, traditionalists on the Pine Ridge Reservation asked for help from AIM (the American Indian Movement). AIM's physical intervention led to the seventy-one-day siege of Wounded Knee in 1973. With international attention now focused on U.S.-Indian relations, the state sought to contain the situation, fighting what Ward Churchill calls a "veritable counterinsurgency war against AIM and the traditional Oglalas of Pine Ridge" (167) that lasted for three years. Sixty AIM members and supporters perished at the hands of Wilson's private army, which was supplied with guns and ammunition by the federal government, and hundreds more were assaulted and harassed. In 1975, an armed confrontation took place between AIM members and the FBI. Thinking they were being attacked by GOON or vigilantes, two members of AIM shot back at and killed two FBI agents, an incident covered in Apted's companion documentary to *Thunderheart, Incident at Oglala*. Jim Vander Wall explains that although the deaths of the two FBI agents were an "unintended consequence," the FBI provoked this firefight in order to justify a "massive paramilitary assault on AIM" (296–97). More than 180 FBI agents descended on Pine Ridge the next day, and, over the next three months, terrorized the population with massive force, including "Huey" helicopters, armored personnel carriers, M-79 grenade launchers, and fixed-wing aircraft. The chairman of the U.S. Civil Rights Commission would later characterize this operation as "an overreaction which takes on aspects of a vendetta . . . a full-scale military type invasion" (letter from Arthur J. Fleming to U.S. Attorney General Edward S. Levi, July 22, 1975, quoted in Vander Wall, 297). The summary I have given here is adapted from Jim Vander Wall, "A Warrior Caged: The Continuing Struggle of Leonard Peltier," and Ward Churchill, "The Earth Is Our Mother," both in *The State of Native America: Genocide, Colonization, and Resistance*, ed. M. Annette Jaimes (Boston: South End, 1992).

23. Smith, "War and Ethnicity," 382.

24. Jimmie Durham, "Cowboys and . . . Notes on Art, Literature, and American Indians in the Modern American Mind," in *The State of Native America: Genocide, Colonization, and Resistance*, ed. M. Annette Jaimes (Boston: South End, 1992): 429.

25. Morson and Emerson, *Mikhail Bakhtin*, 280, 292, 293.

26. Virginia Wright Wexman, *Creating the Couple: Love, Marriage, and Hollywood Performance* (Princeton, N.J.: Princeton University Press, 1993): 75, 76; see in general Wexman's chapter titled "Star and Genre: John Wayne, the Western, and the American Dream of the Family on the Land," 67–129.

27. Smith, "War and Ethnicity," 377, 378.

28. These phrases are found in Hamilton, "Fear and Desire," 16, 23, 18.

29. Ross Gibson, *South of the West: Postcolonialism and the Narrative Construction of Australia* (Bloomington: Indiana University Press, 1992): 12.

30. Wexman, *Creating the Couple*, 77–78.

31. Ibid., 78, 110.

32. Gibson, *South of the West*, 17.

33. Smith, "War and Ethnicity," 391.

34. Richard Slotkin, *Regeneration through Violence: The Mythology of the American Frontier, 1600–1860* (Middletown, Conn.: Wesleyan University Press, 1973). Slotkin argues that the figure of the frontier hunter, who roamed freely over the land rather than cultivating or taking possession of it, became the prototype for the cowboy hero of American myth. The frontiersman, who dominated and subdued the world of nature, was purified by acts of violence, "regenerated" through his violent encounters with game and through his domination of racial others.

35. Robert Stam, Robert Burgoyne, and Sandy Flitterman-Lewis, *New Vocabularies in Film Semiotics* (London: Routledge, 1992): 219.

36. Michael J. Shapiro, "Moral Geographies and the Ethics of Post-Sovereignty," *Public Culture* 6, no. 3 (1994): 485.

37. Walter Benn Michaels, "The Vanishing American," *American Literary History* 2, no. 2 (1990): 233.

3. National Identity, Gender Identity, and the Rescue Fantasy in *Born on the Fourth of July*

1. Susan Jeffords, *The Remasculinization of America: Gender and the Vietnam War* (Bloomington: Indiana University Press, 1989).

2. Stephanie A. Smith, "Heart Attacks: Frederick Douglass's Strategic Sentimentality," *Criticism* 34, no. 2 (1992): 193.

3. Sigmund Freud, "A Special Type of Object Choice Made by Men," in *The Standard Edition of the Complete Psychological Works of Sigmund Freud*, vol. 2, ed. J. Strachey (London: Hogarth, 1962): 163–76.

4. These phrases are from Frederick Douglass, as quoted in Smith, "Heart Attacks."

5. In a recent article, Michael Selig draws attention to numerous analyses based on this premise. See Michael Selig, "Genre, Gender, and the Discourse of War: The A/historical and Vietnam Films," *Screen* 34, no. 1 (1993): 1–18.

6. Laura Mulvey, "Notes on Sirk and Melodrama," in *Home Is Where the Heart Is: Studies in Melodrama and the Woman's Film*, ed. Christine Gledhill (Bloomington: Indiana University Press, 1987): 72.

7. Freud, in "A Special Type of Object Choice," 173, uses these words to describe the emotions associated with the "rescue fantasy." This is in sharp contrast with Selig's statement: "The reconstitution of a heroic male subject, a prerequisite for which is the devaluation and abuse of the feminine" and "their almost always violent repressions of the feminine." "Genre, Gender, and the Discourse of War," 3.

8. See Jean Bethke Elshtain, *Women and War* (New York: Basic Books, 1987). Elshtain asks whether the "current accessibility of the 'Vietnam experience' in and through the language of victimization, estrangement, therapy, and healing will, over time, narrow the gender gap" (220). To which Jeffords replies: "Not moving toward a narrowing of the gender gap . . . the new masculine affirms itself as incorporating, not accepting, the feminine." *The Remasculinization*, 138.

9. Jeffords, *The Remasculinization*, 53.

10. Ibid., 21.

11. Ibid., xiii.

12. Several critics have objected to the characterization of the Vietnam film as a genre, including Linda Dittmar and Gene Michaud, "Introduction—America's Vietnam War Films: Marching toward Denial," in *From Hanoi to Hollywood: The Vietnam War in American Film*, ed. Linda Dittmar and Gene Michaud (New Brunswick, N.J.: Rutgers University Press, 1990): 1–15.

13. George Lipsitz, *Time Passages: Collective Memory and American Popular Culture* (Minneapolis: University of Minnesota Press, 1990): 15.

14. David Grimstead, "Melodrama as Echo of the Historically Voiceless," in *Anonymous Americans: Explorations in Nineteenth Century Social History*, ed. Tamara Hareven (Englewood Cliffs, N.J.: Prentice Hall, 1971): 80, 88.

15. Frank Rahill, *The World of Melodrama* (Philadelphia: University of Pennsylva-

nia Press, 1967); cited in Christine Gledhill, "The Melodramatic Field: An Investigation," in *Home Is Where the Heart Is: Studies in Melodrama and the Woman's Film*, ed. Christine Gledhill (London: British Film Institute, 1987): 25.

16. Robert Stam, Robert Burgoyne, and Sandy Flitterman-Lewis, *New Vocabularies in Film Semiotics: Structuralism, Poststructuralism and Beyond* (London: Routledge, 1992): 219.

17. Gary Saul Morson and Caryl Emerson, *Mikhail Bakhtin: The Creation of a Prosaics* (Stanford, Calif.: Stanford University Press, 1990): 290–92.

18. Ibid., 278.

19. Ibid., 293, 297.

20. Although the historical film has often been denigrated precisely for its melodramatic tendencies—its assimilation of history to "the whole panoply of domestic conflicts" so that "history is shut into that order" (Stephen Heath, "Contexts," *Edinburgh '77 Magazine*, no. 2 [1977]: 42), its inability to depict "social or historical happenings without centering those events around the lives of a few individuals" (David Bordwell, Janet Staiger, and Kristin Thompson, *The Classical Hollywood Cinema: Film Style and Mode of Production to 1960* [Routledge & Kegan Paul, 1985]: 13)—these tendencies are not fatal failings in my view, but rather powerful strategies for questioning an American master narrative that relies for its effectiveness on its reproduction and consolidation in the structures of the family. If the family serves, in the present, as the main conduit of national and political identity, then a genre form traditionally centered on the domestic sphere would seem to be the appropriate vehicle for its analysis and critique.

21. Christine Gledhill, "Between Melodrama and Realism: Anthony Asquith's *Underground* and King Vidor's *The Crowd*," in *Classical Hollywood Narrative: The Paradigm Wars*, ed. Jane M. Gaines (Durham, N.C.: Duke University Press, 1992): 145.

22. Fredric Jameson, "Nostalgia for the Present," in *Postmodernism; or, The Cultural Logic of Late Capitalism* (Durham, N.C.: Duke University Press, 1991): 280.

23. Thomas Elsaesser, "Tales of Sound and Fury," in *Home Is Where the Heart Is: Studies in Melodrama and the Woman's Film*, ed. Christine Gledhill (Bloomington: Indiana University Press, 1987): 61.

24. Gledhill, "Between Melodrama and Realism," 146–47.

25. Elsaesser, "Tales of Sound and Fury," 55.

26. See Smith, "Heart Attacks."

27. P. N. Medvedev, *The Informal Method in Literary Scholarship: A Critical Introduction to Sociological Poetics*, trans. Albert J. Wehrle (Cambridge: Harvard University Press, 1985): 136; quoted in Morson and Emerson, *Mikhail Bakhtin*, 277.

28. Geoffrey Nowell-Smith, "Minnelli and Melodrama," in *Home Is Where the Heart Is: Studies in Melodrama and the Woman's Film*, ed. Christine Gledhill (Bloomington: Indiana University Press, 1987): 72.

29. Aristotle, quoted in ibid.

30. Susan Jeffords, "Can Masculinity Be Terminated?" in *Screening the Male: Exploring Masculinities in Hollywood Cinema*, ed. Steven Cohan and Ina Rae Hark (London: Routledge, 1993): 245–62.

31. Smith, "Heart Attacks," 209.

32. Richard Slotkin, *Regeneration through Violence: The Mythology of the American Frontier, 1600–1860* (Middletown, Conn.: Wesleyan University Press, 1973).

33. Jeffords, "Can Masculinity Be Terminated?" 259.

34. Ina Rae Hark, "Animals or Roman," in *Screening the Male: Exploring Masculinities in Hollywood Cinema*, ed. Steven Cohan and Ina Rae Hark (London: Routledge, 1993): 153.

35. See Steve Neale, "Aspects of Ideology and Narrative Form in the American War Film," *Screen* 32, no. 1 (1991): 35–57.

36. Slotkin, *Regeneration through Violence*, 5.

37. Paul Willeman, "Anthony Mann: Looking at the Male," *Framework* 15–17 (1981): 16.

38. Scott Benjamin King, "Sonny's Virtues: The Gender Negotiations of Miami Vice," *Screen* 31, no. 3 (1990): 292.

39. Steve Neale, "Masculinity as Spectacle," in *Screening the Male: Exploring Masculinities in Hollywood Cinema*, ed. Steven Cohan and Ina Rae Hark (London: Routledge, 1993): 14–15.

40. Hark, "Animals or Roman," 161.

41. Jeffords, "Can Masculinity Be Terminated?" 257–58.

42. For an extended discussion of the use of feminine "types" as images of the national character in the nineteenth century, see Martha Banta, *Imaging American Women: Ideas and Ideals in Cultural History* (New York: Columbia University Press, 1987).

43. As noted previously, the phrases "blood-seeker" and "milk-giver" are from Frederick Douglass, quoted in Smith, "Heart Attacks."

44. Freud, "A Special Type of Object Choice."

45. See Michael Clark, "Remembering Vietnam," in *The Vietnam War and American Culture*, ed. John Carlos Rowe and Rick Berg (New York: Columbia University Press, 1991): 177–207.

46. Rick Berg and John Carlos Rowe, "The Vietnam War and American Memory," in *The Vietnam War and American Culture*, ed. John Carlos Rowe and Rick Berg (New York: Columbia University Press, 1991): 6, 5.

47. Ibid., 6.

48. Ibid.

49. Ibid., 9.

50. Frederick Douglass, *My Bondage and My Freedom*, ed. William Andrews (Urbana: University of Illinois Press, 1987): 225.

51. Berg and Rowe, "The Vietnam War," 4.

52. Clark, "Remembering Vietnam," 204.

53. Miriam Hansen, "The Hieroglyph and the Whore: D. W. Griffith's *Intolerance*," in *Classical Hollywood Narrative: The Paradigm Wars*, ed. Jane M. Gaines (Durham, N.C.: Duke University Press, 1992): 195.

54. Freud, "A Special Type of Object Choice," 173.

55. Ibid.

56. Ibid.

57. Clark, "Remembering Vietnam," 205.

58. Ibid., 203.

59. Freud, "A Special Type of Object Choice," 173.

60. Ibid.

61. Hansen, "The Hieroglyph," 191.

4. Modernism and the Narrative of Nation in *JFK*

1. Oliver Stone and Zachary Sklar, *JFK: The Book of the Film: A Documented Screenplay* (New York: Applause, 1992) contains an extraordinary collection of reviews, commentaries, editorials, and responses constituting several hundred pages, as well as Oliver Stone's and Zachary Sklar's research notes for the film. In addition, *Cineaste* (19,

no. 1 [1992]) has published a special issue on *JFK*, and the April 1992 issue of *American Historical Review* includes a substantial special section on the film. Marjorie Garber, Jann Matlock, and Rebecca Walkowitz's edited collection *Media Spectacles* (New York: Routledge, 1993) contains several chapters that deal with the controversy and debate surrounding *JFK*.

2. Hayden White provides a particularly sophisticated treatment of these issues in relation to *JFK* in "The Fact of Modernism: The Fading of the Historical Event," in *The Persistence of History: Cinema, Television, and the Modern Event*, ed. Vivian Sobchack (New York: Routledge, 1995).

3. Benedict Anderson introduces the term "unisonance" in connection with the singing of the national anthem and the impression of social parallelism and simultaneity it fosters. See *Imagined Communities: Reflections on the Origin and Spread of Nationalism* (London: Verso, 1991): 145.

4. The relation between nationalism and narrative form has been addressed by a number of writers. See, for example, Homi K. Bhabha, "DissemiNation: Time, Narrative, and the Margins of the Modern Nation," and Timothy Brennan, "The National Longing for Form," both in *Nation and Narration*, ed. Homi K. Bhabha (London: Routledge, 1990); William Rowe and Vivian Schelling, *Memory and Modernity: Popular Culture in Latin America* (London: Verso, 1991); Partha Chatterjee, *Nationalist Thought and the Colonial World: A Derivative Discourse* (Minneapolis: University of Minnesota Press, 1993); and Anderson, *Imagined Communities*.

5. Anderson, *Imagined Communities*, 26. The phrase "homogeneous, empty time" comes from Walter Benjamin, *Illuminations* (New York: Schocken, 1969): 261.

6. Anderson, *Imagined Communities*, 25.

7. Ibid.

8. White, "The Fact of Modernism."

9. The phrase "anticipation within retroversion" comes from Mieke Bal, *Narratology: Introduction to the Theory of Narrative* (Toronto: University of Toronto Press, 1985): 67.

10. Brennan, "The National Longing for Form," 49.

11. Renata Wasserman, "Mario Vargas Llosa, Euclides da Cunha, and the Strategy of Intertextuality," *PMLA* (May 1993): 464.

12. See Ann Laura Stoller, "In Cold Blood: Hierarchies of Credibility and the Politics of Colonial Narratives," *Representations* 37 (Winter 1992). The phrase "epistemic murk" comes from Michael Taussig, "Culture of Terror, Space of Death: Roger Casement's Putumayo Report and the Explanation of Torture," *Comparative Studies in Society and History* 26, no. 3 (1984).

13. Homi K. Bhabha, "A Question of Survival: Nations and Psychic States," in *Psychoanalysis and Cultural Theory: Thresholds*, ed. James Donald (London: Macmillan, 1991): 98. Bhabha here explores the limits of Anderson's concept of the unisonance of the imagined community, drawing on competing models of national consciousness as defined by Edward Said and Frantz Fanon.

14. Anderson, *Imagined Communities*, 11. See also Brennan, "The National Longing for Form," 50.

15. The iconography of D.C. monuments has been utilized in other film texts in relation to conspiracy in ways that contrast with *JFK*. In *Mr. Smith Goes to Washington*, for example, the montage elicits a sense of democracy as transparent; in *All the President's Men*, by contrast, the official spaces of Washington are represented as signs that must be deciphered for their underlying, conspiratorial connections. But where *All the President's Men* presents conspiracy as a temporary aberration that can be purged

through the apparatus of "the system" itself, *JFK* narrates a secret history that "derealizes" the dominant historical narrative.

16. In the script of the film, this scene is handled differently. Rather than a black man and his young son at Kennedy's tomb, the script has Garrison flashing back to documentary images of Dachau, with piles of bodies being bulldozed into a ditch. In the logic of the film, this change underlines the message of the importance of national community, associated with the images of Lincoln and Kennedy. It asserts, under the banner of the national, a sense of black and white having a common story and sharing the same fate.

17. Bhabha, "DissemiNation," 297.

18. Rowe and Schelling, *Memory and Modernity*, 204.

19. Ibid., 213.

20. See Dipesh Chakrabarty, "Postcoloniality and the Artifice of History: Who Speaks for 'Indian' Pasts?" *Representations* 37 (Winter 1992). In his concluding paragraphs, Chakrabarty expresses well the dominance of national narratives over other, possible narratives of social connection, and stresses the role of historical writing in furthering this condition.

5. Prosthetic Memory/National Memory: *Forrest Gump*

1. See Michael Kammen, *The Mystic Chords of Memory: The Transformation of Tradition in American Culture* (New York: Knopf, 1991).

2. Thomas Elsaesser, "Subject Positions, Speaking Positions: From *Holocaust, Our Hitler,* and *Heimat* to *Shoah* and *Schindler's List*," in *The Persistence of History: Cinema, Television, and the Modern Event,* ed. Vivian Sobchack (New York: Routledge, 1995): 146.

3. See Walter Benjamin, "The Work of Art in the Age of Mechanical Reproduction," in *Film Theory and Criticism,* ed. Gerald Mast, Marshall Cohen, and Leo Braudy (New York: Oxford University Press, 1994): 665–81.

4. Alison Landsberg, "Prosthetic Memory: The Logics and Politics of Memory in Modern American Culture" (Ph.D. diss., University of Chicago, 1996), abstract: 1.

5. Alison Landsberg, "Prosthetic Memory: *Total Recall* and *Blade Runner*," *Body and Society* 1, nos. 3–4 (1995): 180.

6. Landsberg, "Prosthetic Memory" (diss.), 1.

7. Elsaesser, "Subject Positions," 146.

8. Letter to the editor, *New York Times,* May 10, 1996.

9. Landsberg, "Prosthetic Memory" (diss.), 1.

10. Tom Conley, letter to author, October 15, 1995.

11. See Benedict Anderson, *Imagined Communities: Reflections on the Origin and Spread of Nationalism* (London: Verso, 1991); and Gopal Balakrishnan, "The National Imagination," *New Left Review* 211 (May–June 1995): 56–69.

12. Vivian Sobchack, "Introduction: History Happens," in *The Persistence of History: Cinema, Television, and the Modern Event,* ed. Vivian Sobchack (New York: Routledge, 1995): 2, 3.

13. See Rick Perlstein, "Who Owns the Sixties?" *Lingua Franca* (May/June 1996): 30–37.

Index

Anderson, Benedict, 14, 42, 43, 45, 88–89, 94, 99, 102, 112, 123 (n), 124 (n), 127 (n), 132 (n), 133 (n)
Apocalypse Now, 110
Apted, Michael, 40
Aristotle, 130 (n)

Bakhtin, Mikhail, 7–8, 13, 31, 41, 45, 48, 54, 60, 61, 124 (n), 125 (n), 126 (n), 127 (n), 130 (n)
Bal, Mieke, 132 (n)
Banta, Martha, 131 (n)
Benjamin, Walter, 89, 105, 132 (n), 133 (n)
Berg, Rick, 78, 79, 131 (n)
Berlant, Lauren, 40, 127 (n)
Bhabha, Homi K., 10, 27, 96, 101, 123 (n), 125 (n), 126 (n), 132 (n), 133 (n)
Bordwell, David, 130 (n)
Braudel, Fernand, 44, 127 (n)
Braveheart, 104
Brennan, Timothy, 2, 94, 123 (n), 124 (n), 132 (n)
Burchard, Peter, 126 (n)
Burgoyne, Robert, 129 (n)

Chakrabarty, Dipesh, 133 (n)
Chambers, Ross, 11, 125 (n)
Churchill, Ward, 41, 127 (n), 128 (n)

Clark, Michael, 80, 84, 131 (n)
Colchester, Nicholas, 127 (n)
Conley, Tom, 108, 133 (n)

Dances with Wolves, 39
Dimock, Peter, 17, 125 (n), 127 (n)
Dissanayaka, Wimal, 124 (n), 125 (n)
Dittmar, Linda, 129 (n)
Dominant fiction, 1–3, 15, 17, 36, 121, 123 (n)
Douglass, Frederick, 23, 24–25, 29, 30, 67, 68–69, 79, 126 (n), 129 (n), 131 (n)
Durham, Jimmie, 47, 128 (n)
Dyer, Richard, 18–19, 20, 126 (n)

Elsaesser, Thomas, 65, 66, 104, 106, 130 (n), 133 (n)
Elshtain, Jean Bethke, 129 (n)
Emerson, Caryl, 8, 124 (n), 125 (n), 126 (n), 127 (n), 128 (n), 130 (n)
Emerson, Ralph Waldo, 22, 23

Fanon, Frantz, 27, 126 (n), 132 (n)
Five Hundred Nations, 39
Flitterman-Lewis, Sandy, 129 (n)
Forten, Charlotte, 25, 126 (n)
Freud, Sigmund, 10, 14, 57, 70, 77, 81–82, 86, 122, 129 (n), 131 (n)
Full Metal Jacket, 110

135

Genre memory, 7, 8, 13, 41, 47–48, 61, 124 (n)
Geronimo, 39
Gibson, Ross, 50, 128 (n)
Gilroy, Paul, 17, 32, 34, 125 (n), 126 (n), 127 (n)
Gledhill, Christine, 63, 129 (n), 130 (n)
Grimstead, David, 60, 129 (n)

Hall, Stuart, 33–34, 126 (n)
Hamilton, Annette, 38–40, 42, 124 (n), 125 (n), 127 (n), 128 (n)
Hansen, Miriam, 86, 131 (n)
Hark, Ina Rae, 130 (n), 131 (n)
Huggins, Nathan, 12, 25, 26, 29, 35–36, 124 (n), 125 (n), 126 (n), 127 (n)

Identity from across, 2–3, 13, 17, 36, 75
Ignatieff, Michael, 8, 9, 10, 16, 122, 125 (n)
In the Line of Fire, 82

Jahner, Elaine A., 127 (n)
Jaimes, M. Annette, 128 (n)
James, Caryn, 5, 124 (n)
James, William, 221
Jameson, Fredric, 64, 124 (n), 130 (n)
Jefferson in Paris, 1, 3
Jeffords, Susan, 13, 57, 58–59, 68, 76, 125 (n), 129 (n), 130 (n), 131 (n)

Kammen, Michael, 4, 104, 123 (n), 133 (n)
Kelly, John D., 125 (n)
King, Scott Benjamin, 131 (n)
Krupat, Arnold, 127 (n)

Landsberg, Alison, 105, 133 (n)
Legends of the Fall, 39
Levine, Lawrence, 33, 126 (n)
Lipsitz, George, 4–5, 60, 124 (n), 129 (n)

Malcolm X, 1, 3
Medvedev, Pavel, 67, 130 (n)
Michaels, Walter Benn, 129 (n)
Michaud, Gene, 129 (n)
Morson, Gary Saul, 8, 124 (n), 125 (n), 126 (n), 127 (n), 128 (n), 130 (n)

National imaginary, 12–13, 38–40, 49, 54, 124 (n), 127 (n)

National narrative, 1, 6, 10, 12–14, 21, 22, 27, 37, 40, 60–61, 71, 88, 91, 94, 99–101, 107, 109, 122, 133 (n)
Neale, Steve, 75, 131 (n)
Nixon, 3
Nowell Smith, Geoffrey, 68, 124 (n), 125 (n), 130 (n)

Pearce, Roy Harvey, 45, 123, 127
Perlstein, Rick, 133 (n)
Platoon, 70, 110
Pocahontas, 39
Punitive agency, 14, 57

Rahill, Frank, 60, 129 (n)
Rancière, Jacques, 1–2, 15, 123 (n)
Rescue fantasy, 14, 70, 77, 81–82, 85–86, 129 (n)
Rogin, Michael, 40, 127 (n)
Rowe, John Carlos, 78, 79, 131 (n)
Rowe, William, 132 (n), 133 (n)

Said, Edward, 45, 127 (n)
Scharnhorst, Gary, 126 (n)
Schelling, Vivian, 132 (n), 133 (n)
Schindler's List, 104
Shapiro, Michael J., 129 (n)
Silko, Leslie Marmon, 45
Sklar, Zachary, 131 (n)
Slotkin, Richard, 54, 69, 70, 128 (n), 130 (n), 131 (n)
Smith, Anthony, 8, 9, 10, 46, 49, 54, 124–25 (n), 127 (n), 128 (n)
Smith, Barbara Clark, 127 (n)
Smith, Stephanie, 126 (n), 129 (n), 130 (n), 131 (n)
Sobchack, Vivian, 118–19, 132 (n), 133 (n)
Social memory, 4, 14, 46, 104, 106, 108, 120
Spicer, Edward, 38, 127 (n)
Staiger, Janet, 130 (n)
Stam, Robert, 129 (n)
Stoller, Ann Laura, 132 (n)
Stone, Oliver, 57, 67, 70, 81, 82, 88, 131 (n)

Tamir, Yael, 10, 125 (n)
Taussig, Michael, 132 (n)
Thompson, Kristin, 130 (n)
Turner, Graeme, 11, 125 (n)
Turner, Victor, 6, 124 (n)

Vander Wall, Jim, 128 (n)

Wasserman, Renata, 132 (n)
Way West, The, 39
West, Cornel, 13, 16, 123 (n), 125 (n)
Wexman, Virginia Wright, 3, 48, 50–51,
  123 (n), 128 (n)
White, Armond, 126 (n)

White, Hayden, 14, 89, 94–96, 132 (n)
Willeman, Paul, 70, 131 (n)
Williams, Raymond, 36, 127 (n)
Wood, Peter, 125 (n), 127 (n)
Wounded Knee, 12, 43–44, 46, 51–53,
  121, 128 (n)

Zwick, Edward, 32, 126 (n)

Robert Burgoyne is professor of English and film studies at Wayne State University and chair of the Department of English. His work revolves around issues of historical representation and film, narrative theory and film, and national identity and narrative form. He has published two books, *Bertolucci's 1900: A Narrative and Historical Analysis* (1991), and *New Vocabularies in Film Semiotics: Structuralism, Poststructuralism and Beyond*, which he coauthored (1992). In addition, he has published articles in a number of leading journals, including *Poetique*, *October*, *Film Quarterly*, and *Screen*.